This series offers the concerned reader basic guidelines and *practical* applications of religion for today's world. Although decidedly Christian in focus and emphasis, the series embraces all denominations and modes of Bible-based belief relevant to our lives today. All volumes in the Steeple series are originals, freshly written to provide a fresh perspective on current—and yet timeless—human dilemmas. This is a series of our times. Among the books:

How to Read the Bible
James Fischer

How to Live Your Faith
L. Perry Wilbur

A Spiritual Handbook for Women
Dandi Daley Knorr

Temptation: How Christians Can Deal with It
Frances Carroll

With God on Your Side: A Guide to Finding Self-Worth Through Total Faith
Doug Manning

A Daily Key for Today's Christians: 365 Key Texts of the New Testament
William E. Bowles

How to Talk with God Every Day of the Year:
A Book of Devotions for Twelve Positive Months
Frances Hunter

Walking in the Garden: Inner Peace from the Flowers of God
Paula Connor

How to Bring Up Children in the Catholic Faith
Carol and David Powell

Sex in the Bible: An Introduction to What the Scriptures Teach Us About Sexuality
Michael R. Cosby

God's Conditions for Prosperity: How to Earn the Rewards of Christian Living
Charles Hunter

Pilgrimages: A Guide to the Holy Places of Europe for Today's Traveler
Paul Lambourne Higgins

Journey into the Light: Lessons of Pain and Joy to Renew Your Energy and Strengthen Your Faith
Dorris Blough Murdock

A CHILD OF GOD

Activities for Teaching Spiritual Values to Children of All Ages

Peggy D. Jenkins

A SPECTRUM BOOK

Prentice-Hall, Inc., Englewood Cliffs, New Jersey 07632

Library of Congress Cataloging in Publication Data

Jenkins, Peggy Davison.
  A child of God.

  (Steeple books)
  Rev. ed. of: Climbing the rainbow, 1983.
  "A Spectrum Book."
  Includes index.
  1. Religious education of young people.   2. Youth—
Religious life.   I. Jenkins, Peggy Davison.   Climbing the
rainbow.   II. Title.   III. Series.
BL42.J46 1984   207   84-3322
ISBN 0-13-130857-2
ISBN 0-13-130840-8 (pbk.)

10 9 8 7 6 5 4 3 2 1

ISBN 0-13-130857-2

ISBN 0-13-130840-8 {PBK.}

Previously published as *Climbing the Rainbow: Teaching Spiritual Object
Lessons*, Unity Village, MO: The Association of Unity Churches Youth
Services and Coleman Publishing, 1983.

Editorial/production supervision: Marlys Lehmann
Cover design: Hal Siegel
Manufacturing buyer: Doreen Cavallo

This book is available at a special discount when ordered in
bulk quantities. Contact Prentice-Hall, Inc., General
Publishing Division, Special Sales, Englewood Cliffs, N.J. 07632.

Prentice-Hall International, Inc., *London*
Prentice-Hall of Australia Pty. Limited, *Sydney*
Prentice-Hall Canada Inc., *Toronto*
Prentice-Hall of India Private Limited, *New Delhi*
Prentice-Hall of Japan, Inc., *Tokyo*
Prentice-Hall of Southeast Asia Pte. Ltd., *Singapore*
Whitehall Books Limited, *Wellington, New Zealand*
Editora Prentice-Hall do Brasil Ltda., *Rio de Janeiro*

Contents

To the children of the world,
that they may save time
on our journey homeward.

It is written that only
as one become as the little child
shall one enter the portals
of wisdom.

Preface

With a background of mother, parent/teacher educator, and student of spiritual/metaphysical principles, it seemed only logical to bring these fields together in the hope of accelerating the consciousness growth the world needs.

As a parent I felt a great need for more material on the mental and spiritual laws that was in a form easy to share with children. The result was the combining of three of my favorite teaching tools: truth principles, visual aids, and analogies.

The saying that we teach what we need to learn never felt truer to me than when writing this book. I am joyous about sharing it with you, that it might help you as it has helped me. It is certainly not a book just for children, but for the child in each of us.

It is my loving hope that you and the children on your path have a glorious time on your journey homeward.

Great truths are dearly bought,
The common truth,
Such as men give and take from day to day,
Comes in the common walk of easy life,
Blown by the careless wind across our way.

Great truths are greatly won, not found by chance,
Nor wafted on the breath of summer's dream;
But grasped in the great struggle of the soul,
By hard buffeting with adverse wind and stream.

—Unknown

First I must acknowledge the powerful guidance of the set of books called *A Course in Miracles*.

Next, I owe a debt of gratitude to the great many ministers, teachers, and authors who have provided the inspiration for the lessons in this book. Over years of study, the ideas and sources have blended into a whole, making it difficult for me to give isolated credit. Nevertheless, my gratitude goes to everyone who contributed to this work.

My very special thanks to Char Webster for her invaluable suggestions and editing help.

Appreciation goes to Sandra Pezoldt and Gina Griffin for the many hours of art lovingly contributed to this project.

Unity Church and Coleman Publishing each have my deep gratitude for their vision in printing the earlier edition of this book, titled *Climbing the Rainbow: Teaching Spiritual Object Lessons*.

Nothing of this nature is ever achieved alone, so I acknowledge with great appreciation all the "Invisible Help" that was received, by whatever name you choose to call it.

Laying the Foundation

A goal of this book is to help young people start believing the things that are true about themselves. When they know the truth about themselves, as children of God, fantastic things begin to happen to them and to their world. They will provide the leadership needed to bring in the New Age.

Someone once said, "Woe to the man who has to learn principles in the time of crisis." The principles that children will learn in this book will help prepare them for whatever they may encounter in life. This is because they will come to understand that this is a mental and spiritual world, and whatever is in their lives is but the material expression of a belief in their minds. There is much backward thinking that sees the outside world as cause and ourselves as effect. It is hoped that they will come to see themselves as cause and the world as effect. The sound self-esteem that will result from working with these principles will help youngsters in whatever situations they may find themselves.

For every physical law, there is a parallel law in mind and spirit. Why not teach children to work with the spiritual laws as well as the physical? This will bring with it the gifts of peace, security, and confidence that will enable them to weather the storms of life.

The lessons that follow are simply to start the process. They are intended as aids for busy parents who are willing to take five minutes a day to teach some higher principles to their children. Many teachers, ministers, and counselors will find them usable, too. By no means does this group of lessons represent all the principles that need to be taught. They are simply those that meet the criteria of being quick to teach with household objects at the level of understanding of most school-age children.

The emphasis is on kitchen objects, as the lessons in the home would most likely take place there. Objects have long been a successful way of using the familiar to make clear the unfamiliar.

The highest kinds of learning are in symbols, not words, and easy-to-understand objects can symbolize many hard-to-understand truths.

Kahlil Gibran tells us, "Faith perceives Truth sooner than experience can." Your children may be short on experience but long on faith. You, as an adult, do not need to know all the answers to use these lessons. Just set the stage and tickle the children with these concepts which their own Inner Teacher can mold into perfect understanding.

Throughout each lesson it is of utmost importance to build the child's self-esteem. Never is the goal of the lesson more important than the feelings of the child. Always help the child to feel good about him or herself.

You certainly do not have to be in full agreement with what is offered here; but if the ideas trigger your thinking and give you other ideas for teaching truths that are meaningful to you, the book will have served its purpose.

How to Use This Book

Most of the lessons can be accomplished in five minutes or so. For parents, adding the time to the morning schedule is suggested, as it is desirable to begin the child's day with this kind of food for thought. The mind, as well as the body, needs to be nourished. Or a parent may wish to use the lessons at bedtime or after school. The important thing is to have a regular schedule and to be consistent.

As there is no necessary sequence to the lessons, you may treat the book as a smorgasbord and pick and choose lessons depending on the needs of your children and your own interests. Watch for the "teachable moments."

The lessons are not written to be read to the child. They are for the adult to read and adapt to the child's level of understanding, augmented with personal examples.

It is better to cut the lessons short, leaving the child wanting a little more, than to exhaust the subject and bore the child. Studies with young children show that there is greater retention when a task is left incomplete. Rather than milk the analogy dry, just plan to revisit the idea occasionally.

The best formula for utilizing any of these lessons is KISS (Keep It Short and Simple). It will make a more lasting impression. The child's mind really doesn't need a lot of words and explanations. It is the adult mind that demands this.

The recommended procedure is to have the objects for the lesson already sitting on the table when the child arrives. This will intrigue him and build interest, maybe even suspense. Add a bit to the drama by having a special tray or mat on which the objects are placed. A most effective way to enhance the drama is to use a puppet or two to help teach the lesson.

There are lessons here for different levels of awareness. Make it okay to skip over any that do not appeal to you. If a lesson is not entirely accurate according to your philosophy, feel free to alter it or eliminate it. It is much better to teach the lessons you are excited about. This kind of enthusiasm is contagious. With children, often, much more is "caught than taught."

These lessons are designed to be adaptable to any age group from elementary through high school. Even if young people of diverse age groups are hearing a lesson together, they will each "get it" at their level of understanding. That is why specific scripts or explanations at the child's level are left out. You are then free to offer explanations that correspond to your level of metaphysical understanding.

It is urged that you read the lesson at least two days ahead of time, for a couple of reasons. One is so that you can be sure to have on hand whatever is needed. Most items are common to every household, but now and then there are a few exceptions. The other reason is that by reading the lessons ahead, you give your subconscious mind valuable time with the idea. You'll have a deeper understanding of it by the time of the lesson and, perhaps, a more meaningful way to present the idea. You can invite the creative subconscious mind to provide you with specific examples that your child will relate to. Please keep in mind that this material is intended to be open-ended so that you can take off with it in a way that is most in keeping with your belief system, while best meeting the needs of the children.

You may wish to end the lesson with an affirmation for each child or with a group affirmation. Affirmations are positive declarations of Truth and, as such, are powerful tools for changing one's thinking and attitudes, hence, one's experience. They are more fully explained in the section "Guidelines for Affirmations." In this case, the affirmation should be an outgrowth of each lesson. It can directly reinforce the lesson or relate to some concern of the child's which was revealed in the discussion of the lesson. Repeated use of the affirmation throughout the day can bring the child closer to the real truth about him or herself.

Another suggestion is to be sure to allow time for input and questions from the children. Try not to make the lesson a straight monologue. Often children are closer to the "Truth" than we are and can teach us with their keen insights. Be willing to reverse roles and be the learner. It has been well said that "we teach what we are and what others are to us."

There are many times when it is impossible or totally inappropriate to use the objects involved in a lesson, but you still desire to get the message across. The next best thing to using objects is to paint a word picture. A picture in the mind can make a much more lasting impression than words without a visual image. For instance, a child can easily visualize a wastebasket of debris and a gift package hidden inside it (Lesson 32). A visual picture like that will more readily come to mind when needed than just eloquent words, such as, "There is the seed of advantage within every disadvantage." Of course, the actual "hands-on" experience with objects themselves will always make the strongest impression.

Another way of impressing the mind is through repetition. A principle may need to be repeated many times before it is heard. Do not hesitate to repeat lessons every so often. Many of the lesson are simply different ways of saying the same thing, and that is effective teaching.

To make the book a more effective teaching tool, it is suggested that you maintain a notebook to record ideas before, during, or after the lesson. This could be a useful record of your additions, alterations, examples, affirmation ideas, and the response or questions of the children. You may wish to jot down plans for augmenting the lesson, such as role-playing, meditations, and art and science projects. It is always helpful to record how a lesson went over and to make suggestions for using it next time.

Perhaps the greatest contribution these lessons can make will be to trigger similar ideas in your mind to better portray your philosophy. It is hoped that these activities will be a jumping-off place, and that you'll start seeing in everyday objects a great many ways to expand children's understanding of this mental and spiritual universe.

Guidelines
for Affirmations

An affirmation concludes each lesson, so it is suggested that this section be read before beginning the lessons.

Affirmations, as used in this book, are positive statements about who we are and what we can become or experience.

What needs to be expanded are our beliefs about ourselves. We need to bring our self-awareness into harmony with the divine perfection that already exists within us.

All our beliefs are stored in the subconscious area of our minds. They are comprised of emotions, fears, doubts, actual happenings, and the accepted opinion of others. The lower or negative beliefs can be replaced by higher level or spiritual beliefs. This is where the tool of affirmation comes in. Because we are spirit, we are, in essense, perfect. We have a right to call forth that perfection by believing in it and speaking the word.

Of course, there are negative affirmations which we have unconsciously used all our lives, bringing about many unwanted conditions. We affirm negatively when we say,"I can't do this," "I'm so tired," "I think I'm getting sick," "I'm such a slow reader," "I am lousy at spelling," or "My memory is poor." Most of the time this kind of affirming, or self-negation, is carried on silently in our "self-talk," that steady stream of internal verbalization.

Anything we really want to change about ourselves can be changed by the use of positive declarations or affirmations. Words clothed with feeling have the power to impregnate the subconscious mind. It is the process of osmosis, as a stalk of celery turns red when left sitting in red-colored water or a white carnation is dyed blue when left in a dish of blue water. Other useful analogies are used in the lesson "The Power of Affirmations."

With young children, affirmations work very rapidly because children are closer to the truth about themselves. They have not had as many years of brainwashing to the contrary as have most adults.

Affirmations must be believable to the conscious mind before they will be fully accepted by the subconscious mind. The subconscious phase of mind is the formative power, and it will give form to what we feel is true for us now. It is the feelings that form, not the words alone.

Suggestions for
Forming Affirmations

1. Make the affirmation personal by using "I" or "My" or your name. Powerful affirmations begin with "I am." "I can" affirmations are also very effective. Use your name in the affirmation when possible." "I (name) am a good swimmer."

2. Word your affirmation as if you had already made the change you want to make—as if you were already the kind of person you want to be.

3. Use present tense, because future tense can destroy the value of an affirmation. The subconscious mind is very literal, and, if your affirmation is worded to take place in the future, it will always be in the future. So avoid "I will . . . ," "I am getting . . . ," and similar statements.

4. The affirmation should indicate that the result has been achieved, not that you are "growing into it." Affirmations work best if accompanied by a visualization. It is easier to picture an accomplished fact than a vague process of growth.

5. The affirmation should describe the attitudes you wish to cultivate and not what you want to move away from. Instead of "I don't lose my temper," say, "I am even-tempered."

6. Do not compare yourself with others in your affirmation,

such as, "I can write as well as Susan." Focus on you, "I express myself clearly."

7. Be specific as to the exact level you want to achieve. "I can swim three laps of the pool." "I play this week's piano lesson perfectly."

8. Inject feeling words into your affirmations to give them an emotional charge. For example, "I enjoy doing math," or, "I am proud of the fact that I am a good pianist."

Suggestions for the Use of Affirmations

- Affirmations impress the subconscious mind most powerfully when used in a very relaxed state, such as when falling asleep, when waking up, or in a meditative state. That is why negative thoughts held at such times can do so much damage.

- It is extremely effective to have a mental picture accompany the affirmation. A strong picture can be worth 1,000 words. Our formative subconscious is very receptive to detailed visualization.

- The more joyous the emotion one attaches to the affirmation, the more effective it will be. Feelings, both negative and positive, have formative powers.

- Repetition is another key to successful affirming. Use it many times a day. Displaying it in several places can be a helpful reminder.

- The more senses you involve, the more power you will add to the affirmation. Writing it, speaking it aloud, and even chanting or singing it are recommended for rapid results.

Further Suggestions

The most important affirmations you can get children to use are those that build self-esteem. Self-esteem is the foundation of a happy, successful life. Many parents and teachers teach their small children to use the magic words "I like myself" many times a day. The friendliness and cooperation such words foster is amazing to those who don't understand that you can't like others unless you like yourself.

Older children can use "I feel warm and loving toward myself, or, "I love myself totally and completely." Of course, the self being referred to is the Higher Self. They are loving the Spirit within them. As already stated, the use of affirmations is most effective when waking of falling asleep. They help counteract the bombardment of self-inflicted put-down many experience throughout the day.

It is strongly suggested that the parent or teacher use affirmative prayer for the success of the day's object lesson. Write or say: The mind and heart of this child is open to receive the lesson at his or her own level of understanding.

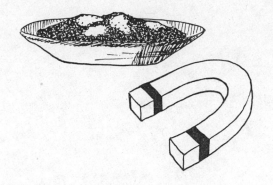

1

The Magnetism
of Praise

Materials

Saucer of sand, magnet or two. (Salt may be substituted.)

Lesson

Ask the children if they can pick out the tiny particles of iron that are in the sand with their eyes or their fingers. Ask what tool could help them do that. Bring forth a magnet and watch the specks of iron stick to it. (Try it out ahead of time and make sure you have sand with some iron in it. If necessary, this can be created by filing an iron nail.)

Tell the children that the saucer of sand represents their day and the magnet represents a thankful heart. A thankful heart can scan one's day and pick out many blessings, just as the magnet can pick out the iron.

Compare the ungrateful heart to our fingers that can search and search through the sand (our day) and not find any iron particles (anything to praise).

The heart that is full of thankfulness and praise will find in every hour of the day something to be grateful for. Suggest taking turns picking up some grains of sand with the magnet and pretend that they are the blessings each one has had that very hour. Friends, eyesight, hearing, good breakfast, nice clothing, may be some examples they will offer.

Then another sweep through with the magnet can pick up blessings from the previous hour. Such things as a compliment, family members, playthings, and pets might be volunteered. Continue on to the night before or the previous day.

Explain that whenever they show gratitude for what is in their life, it works like a magnet and draws more good to them. This appreciation may be silent and may take the form of silently praising the fine qualities they see in others. Such praise will magnetize those qualities to them and they'll have even more to be thankful for.

This analogy could be applied to a current challenge in the child's life, such as a move to a new state or a broken leg. The saucer of sand would represent the situation, the magnet would be the mind that searches for the good in it, and the iron particles would be the blessings the child can discover.

Note: An additional analogy could be used by bringing out a magnifying glass and explaining that God magnifies what we praise and bless. Those blessings represented by the grains of sand will increase when we have a truly thankful heart.

Suggested Affirmation

I am a grateful person and I enjoy praising the good in my life.

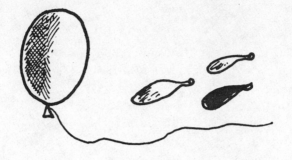

2

The Inside
Gives Form
to the Outside

Materials

One balloon already blown up, and three or four extra balloons; could have balloon for each child (optional).

Lesson

The balloons represent people—each one an individual person. State that each person is filled with the breath of life just like the balloons. Suggest that a child blow up a balloon by filling it with his or her breath of life. Help them to see that this same air or life is in all balloons and all people.

People only see the outside of the balloon or the outside of people, and they tend to think that's the important part. What's really important, however, is what is on the inside, because what's on the inside creates the outside. It's the inside that gives form to the balloon. Otherwise, it would be limp and useless like an uninflated balloon (show example).

We need to see the insides of others as more important than their outside forms. Of course, the air inside us is important because it is what gives us life. Also important, inside us, are our thoughts and attitudes. In many ways these help shape us and our experiences. But what is really important is the Christ within. You may prefer other terminology, such as Holy Spirit or God, for that point of perfection that all people share despite appearances.

Continue with the balloon analogy as follows: "Can you see that the life or air on the inside of the balloon is the important part?" Ask the child what happens to it when you release the air from the balloon. They'll see that the air rejoins the larger body of air outside it. You may then choose to compare this release of life/air to the death of the body. Help them see that there is no real death because the life force rejoins its source just like the air, and continues on in a different form. If there has been a recent death in the family, this could be a most helpful lesson.

Suggested Affirmation

I remember that what's inside people is more important than what's outside.

3

We Are
a Visible Form
of Spirit

Bowl of cold water with ice cubes in it.

Explain that the ice cubes represent us (all people), and the water in the bowl represents Spirit, the invisible power of the universe. Through a certain process, water can take form—the form of ice. Spirit, which is invisible, can also take form and become visible. We are visible forms of Spirit, just as the ice cubes are a form of the water.

It is important to remember that the ice cubes originally came from the water, and not the water from the ice cubes. We came forth from the invisible to the visible. As when the ice melts and becomes water once again, at the time of so-called death, we simply lay aside our bodies and our spirits return to Spirit, or the so-called invisible.

To allay fears about being invisible or "nothing," explain that they'll be in a world which will be very happy and comfortable and visible to them. They'll simply be in spiritual bodies instead of physical bodies. You might explain that some people aren't immediately aware that they have left the physical body when they have made the transition called death. Consider looking into some of the current books by research doctors who are writing on life after death.

You might end the lesson with the explanation that just all is energy, but it changes form just as water can change from liquid to steam or ice. A steaming tea kettle on the stove can emphasize this change of form.

Suggested Affirmation

I am spirit.

4

Prayer Makes the Day

A loosely woven piece of fabric about six inches square or larger. One edge should be hemmed, and the opposite edge fringed a bit. Optional idea: an unhemmed piece of cloth for each child, plus needle and thread.

_____Lesson_____

This lesson is based on a quote from an unknown author: "A day hemmed with prayer is less likely to unravel."

You might begin by pointing out how the hem is preventing the edge of the cloth from unraveling. Pull a loose thread from the opposite end to show what can happen when there is no hem. You can even compare a fully hemmed piece of fabric with a completely unhemmed piece after each has gone through the washing machine.

The hem represents prayer, especially early morning prayer. The fabric is our day, and the unraveled edge of the fabric represents the troubles, irritants, and mistakes that can occur in one's day. The children can offer examples of a day that is full of "goofs."

Offer examples of prayer that can be used to start a day off on the right footing. This can include asking God to guide the day, affirming divine order for the day, affirming to be of help to others, affirming a state of peace and love no matter what occurs. With needle and thread each child might hem his or her piece of cloth as affirmative prayer thoughts are contributed or spoken in unison.

Here you can also discuss the powerful techniques of visualizing a happy day. Be sure to take some time to actually pray together and give thanks for God's guidance in all areas of life.

Suggested
Affirmation

I start my day with prayer and let God lead the way.

5

Spirit Is
Everywhere Present

Materials

Loaf of bread; pieces of various sizes and shapes torn off from it.

Lesson

Give each youngster a piece of bread. Your dialogue might follow along these lines: "Do your pieces look the same? Even though they are different sizes and shapes, what is the same about them?" Help them to see that they are all identical in the ingredients that go to make up each chunk of bread. One doesn't have more salt, another more flour.

Explain that the pieces of bread are just like them. Each is made up of the same basic stuff even though their shapes and sizes are different. The loaf of bread represents Spirit or God and, since Spirit is everywhere present, it is in each of them. They all are a small part of Spirit and so have within them the God qualities of perfect peace, love, health, order, wisdom, and so forth.

Discuss how this is true of everybody in the world, no matter what they look like or act like. Each has the qualities of Spirit inside. Sometimes these are well hidden because the person doesn't know about them. We can help such people by looking for the love, peace, order, health, and goodness that we know is in them. There is no separation. We are all part of the One.

There is not a spot where God is not.

6

Like
Attracts
Like

Materials

A strong magnet or two; two bits of paper and pieces of tape; a tray of small objects, some containing iron or steel. Test beforehand to be sure the magnet will pick up a number of items. Know which ones these are. Most of the objects for the tray can be found quickly by a trip around the kitchen (paper cup, straw, toothpicks, pencil, paper clip, measuring spoon, potato peeler, jar lid, bottle opener, nail, spice can, scissors, egg timer, nut cracker, scouring pad, salt shaker, and so forth). You may wish to let the children experiment first to see which items the magnet will attract. If they don't know it, point out the common denominator of these objects—iron.

Lesson

Your dialogue could run like this:

"There is a law of mind that says 'like attracts like.' It's called the law of attraction or magnetism. Let me show you how it works. We'll pretend that these items are all thoughts, including this magnet. Let's say that this magnet is a happy thought. (Label it with a slip of paper.) It thinks, 'I have so many neat friends.' Now here are two objects; one is a happy thought, "I'm a good singer' (hold up a magnetic object), and the other is sad, "I'm awful at sports' (hold up a non-magnetic object). Which thought do you think this magnetic thought will attract? (Wait for response.) Remember the law is "like attracts like." Sure enough, it attracted the happy thought. Let's see if it happens again. These are the thoughts: "Teacher likes me," and "My brother is mean." Sure enough, it attracted the positive thought. (Remove objects from the tray as they are used.)

"Now let's take the other magnet (if there are two) or change the name of this one and label it an unhappy thought. Maybe it's, "Poor me, nobody played with me at school today." What kind of thoughts do you think it will attract? Remember the law. Can you name some unhappy thoughts? Each of those unhappy thoughts will attract another one (demonstrate with magnet and other objects). People thinking happy thoughts will attract to them-selves happy, positive people that are fun to be around. If they keep thinking unhappy thoughts, they will attract other negative people and ideas. That's the way the law of attraction works."

Suggested
Affirmation

I am a happy person and attract only good to myself.

7

The Power
of Affirmations

Materials

Clear glass, three-quarters full of water; bottle of blue (or any color) food coloring; spoon; bleach in small glass; eye dropper (straw can be used in lieu of eye dropper). For alternative analogy, have on hand a glass of small pebbles or beans.

Lesson

(Best used after "Like Attracts Like" Lesson.)

Let the glass represent a person's mind, and the water the thoughts held in the mind. Point out how this mind right now is full of clear, clean thoughts. Elicit examples of the positive, happy kinds of thoughts that this water might represent. Have the children put in a drop of food coloring and call it a negative thought. Ask the children what it might be and have a suggestion yourself. (Examples: "I can't speak in front of other people"; "What dumb ideas I have.") You might say, "Oops! Here comes another negative thought" (as you add another drop of food coloring). What do you suppose attracted these thoughts?— "I'm such a slowpoke," "Other people are much better at things than I am." Help the children remember the "like attracts like" law and that a negative thought will draw to it more negative thoughts.

Repeat the process of adding negativity until the water is a medium blue. Have the children think of prevalent negative statements heard at school or on TV.

Explain that the person with a mind full of negativity is probably feeling rather tired. It has been found that people burn physical energy three times faster when thinking negatively than when thinking positively.

Ask the children if they have any ideas about how one can get rid of all that negativity in the mind—all those fear, doubt, and limitation thoughts. If they don't know about affirmations, teach them about these positive statements that can work amazingly for them (see "Guidelines for Affirmations"). Explain that it often takes many of these positive thoughts to cancel out a negative thought. This is because the negative has usually been put in with so much more feeling or emotion.

Let the colored water represent one particular fear or limitation they may feel. Make up an affirmation to counteract it, and have them add a drop of bleach to the water. Have the children repeat the affirmation or similar ones while they add another drop of bleach each time. (Example: For a fear of being dumb or not as capable as others—"I am a smart person"; "I have lots of ability"; "I am a fast learner.") Stir the water now and then to mix in the bleach, and repeat until water is back to its clear, positive condition.

An alternative analogy to show power of affirmation: Use a full glass of water and enough small pebbles or dried beans to fill the glass. Compare the negativity stored in our minds to the water in the glass, and have the pebbles represent affirmations that can displace that negativity. Larger pebbles or beans can be used for affirmations put in (stated) with great emotion or feeling. Again, a particular limiting thought can be used, and the pebbles can represent specific affirmations. For instance, if the lack is friends, affirmations can be along the lines of: "New friends are continually coming into my life," "I am a warm and loving person," "I am responsive to other people's needs," "I have friends by being one," "There is an abundance of friends in my life."

Suggested Affirmation

I can choose how I want to feel by the way I think and talk.

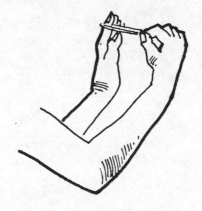

The Boomerang Law

Materials

A rubber band. Optional props that could enhance this lesson are: a boomerang, a Yo-Yo, a party horn that unrolls when blown and then rolls back up, or a Chinese Yo-Yo.

Lesson

The Boomerang Law is another name for the Law of Cause and Effect—the basic universal law that is known by so many labels. The aim of this lesson is to remind us that we will reap what we sow.

Have the children observe while you put a rubber band around your finger, stretch it out and let it lightly snap back a few times. The Law of Cause and Effect says that what goes out, comes back—just like the rubber band. Whatever is put into the universe, in the way of thought, word, or action, travels back to the central point that sent it out. If one sends out friendly thoughts and actions, one will attract friendliness from others. Pull the rubber band to represent a friendly thought about someone. Now let it lightly snap back to represent good returning as a result of the friendly thought. Next have the children choose a critical thought, pull the rubber band out, and let it snap back to indicate that criticism will also return.

If you have a Chinese Yo-Yo or a regular Yo-Yo, you can toss the Yo-Yo out and name a positive thought like love. As the Yo-Yo returns you can say love again, to represent love coming back. You may repeat this with a negative example as well.

"As ye sow, so shall ye reap" is another way of stating this universal law. If we are sharing and helpful, we'll find people eager to share with us and give a hand. If we hold fearful thoughts or act as if we are afraid of getting hurt or losing something, sure enough those kinds of experiences will come into our world.

End on a positive note by emphasizing the children's fantastic, creative nature and their ability to choose what comes into their lives by choosing their thoughts and actions.

Suggested Affirmation

Only good goes from me; only good comes to me.

9

Think About
What You Want,
Not What
You Don't Want

Materials

Two drinking glasses about two-thirds full of caked-on dirt; spoon; bowl; sink with running water.

Lesson

Explain that we are the glass, and the dirt represents a negative condition or problem in our lives. We can clean out this problem in either of two ways.

One is by digging at it and scraping it out, which is what we do when we concentrate on the problem, trying to solve it. Scrape the dirt into a bowl, showing how the glass still isn't very clean.

Show that the other way is much easier because all you have to do is place the glass of dirt under a water faucet and let the water run on it for about five minutes. Do so.

The water represents prayer, a flow of positive thoughts and mental pictures that concentrate only on the desired result, giving no thought to the problem. The full attention is put on the end result, not on the means of getting it. The positive thoughts are best stated as affirmations. This method washes the problem away effortlessly, without struggle. If outer action is needed, we will receive that guidance in prayer.

While the glass is getting clean or clear of the problem, encourage specific examples on the part of the children. Name a problem familiar to them, and get affirmation and mental picture suggestions that can be used to wash it away. You may also wish to reverse the process. Display a clear glass of water (representing the children full of positive thoughts), and show how cloudy it can get with the introduction of even a small amount of negative thinking (dirt).

Suggested Affirmation

I keep my attention on the happy and good.

10

What Gets
My Attention
Gets Me

Container such as bud vase, or pop or ketchup bottle, thin wire, scissors or wire snips, assortment of objects such as can of soup, spice jars, salt and pepper shakers, cup, bar of soap. Extend the wires from the neck of the vase to the various objects. If necessary, use tape to connect them. (String could be substitued for wire.)

Lesson

Begin the lesson by saying that the vase represents us and the wires represent our attention. There is a spiritual law that says, "What you put your attention on you connect with, and the essence of it comes back to you on your attention. Where your attention goes, energy flows."

So if your attention settles on something you don't want in your life (run finger along wire to one of the objects), what you need to do is snip that wire. Think of this as a telephone wire that can send messages back and forth. If the wire is cut, there are no more messages. (Snip the wire.)

Suggest that the objects are representing situations that could have gotten our attention in a negative way. Give an example of your own. For instance, "I was thinking today about how critical Mrs. G is. It seems as if nothing ever pleases her. She criticizes everything. If I dwell on the way she criticizes, I'll draw more of it to me—other critical people or a critical attitude in myself. So what I want to do is quickly snip that wire of attention (snip a wire) and free myself from that negativity.

"Now, let's have an example of something *you* might have put your attention on that you wouldn't want in your life." As examples are offered, assign one to each object that has a wire attached. Snip the wire as the law is restated (what you put your attention on comes back to you).

Examples that could come forth from the children: Daddy not finding a job, fighting on TV, the chores I don't like to do, someone stealing my bike, not having spending money like the other kids, being a slow reader—the list is endless.

Suggest that anytime they're aware of their attention being on something they don't want in their life, they can mentally snip the wire and quickly think about what they do want. Explain that our feelings are the key to our attention. They are more powerful than thought; they carry more energy.

You might add another object and connect a wire to it also. Say that this represents God, the good. If they contemplate the love, wisdom, and power of God, the same law will attract these qualities to them. What gets our attention gets us—so let's put it on the highest thought, God.

You might end the lesson having wire taped to several new objects, each one representing a positive idea the children would want to keep their attention on, such as friendships, health, good grades, learning a new skill, and so forth.

Suggested Affirmation

I keep my attention on the positive and good.

Thoughts
Don't Leave
Their Source

Materials

For each child, plus the adults, have a pencil, paper clip, carbon paper, and two sheets of typing paper. Place the carbon paper face down between the two sheets of typing paper and paper clip them together. Before inserting the carbon, write in the corner of the top sheet the words "Other People," and "My Body and Brain" on the bottom sheet.

Lesson

Have the children think of some happy and unhappy thoughts of the past several days. Encourage an awareness of both loving, kind thoughts and hateful, angry, resentful thoughts that they have had toward others. To aid the memory process, provide some real-life examples of your own. With each one you recall, write the word on your paper. Have the children do the same, using symbols instead of words if writing doesn't come easily. For instance, a circle could stand for a love feeling, and a scribble for an angry feeling.

After the list is completed, look at the bottom sheet of paper where all the marks have been duplicated. Point out how all our thoughts and feelings left their marks on our bodies and brains. They didn't just leave us and go out to the other person. Explain, at each child's level, that the vibrations of the emotions affect our bodies and that thought makes an impression in our brains, which affects the way we see our world. Therefore, we can never give hurtful or hateful thoughts away. Whatever we're feeling is affecting us more than the other person. Sometimes the other person isn't even aware of our feelings. Whatever we give, the good and the bad, is given to ourselves.

One way to release the negative is through the use of denials and affirmations such as suggested at the end of this lesson. Also, we can help ourselves by thinking happy, kind, loving thoughts because they have a healing and harmonizing effect on the body. You may wish to end the lesson by both children and adults putting on the paper some positive thoughts about specific people and then observing how these emotions were recorded on the body/brain sheet.

Suggested Affirmation

(Denial) *I release all thoughts that are harmful to me and others.*

(Affirmation) *I am careful to think thoughts that help me and others.*

12

Do Your Words Have Weights or Wings?

Two pieces of paper or cardboard folded in half to make stand-up signs. Print "Feel Good" on one sign and "Feel Bad" on the other; pile of single words cut out of a newspaper or magazine. If children are participating, not just observing, have about a dozen per child.

Lesson

Our words may weigh others down or lift them up. They can help others to feel bad or to feel good. The same idea applies to our thoughts because words are just symbols of thoughts. Have the children place the words in front of them and form an arrow with them. Usually everything we say points toward either a good feeling or a bad feeling. They might shift their arrows in the direction of the appropriate sign as sample statements are offered.

The words that lead toward Feel Bad are the words that weigh people down and make them feel heavy, discouraged, limited, lacking, or fearful in some way. This includes not just put-downs but the reporting of negative news, criticism, probing, or anything that creates the illusion of separation between people. All words that point toward Feel Bad are a form of separation because they ignore that the other person is also a Holy Son or Daughter of God.

Words that point toward Feel Good are sincere words that lift people, lighten them, make them feel capable, lovable, and positive. Such words make people feel good about themselves, others, and about their world. Feel Good words bring light into the mind and heart, while words pointing toward Feel Bad bring darkness.

Suggest that they become careful observers of people's reactions, so that they will know how other people are responding to their words.

The focus has been on the effect of words or thoughts on others. Make sure the children understand that their own words can also have a powerful effect on themselves. If they're thinking gloom and doom thoughts, being critical of themselves, speaking of lack or limitation, they are creating darkness instead of light in their minds.

This session might end with participants speaking to each other, using only words with wings—words that uplift.

Suggested
Affirmation

My words have wings; they are uplifting.

13

Only Our Thoughts
Hurt Us

Materials

Pencils and small pieces of paper for each participant; three boxes about the same size (small cereal, pudding, or gelatin boxes would work well for a small group of children). Tape a piece of paper with the word "Experience" on the side of one box; a piece with the word "Unhappiness" on another box, and "Happiness" on the reverse side of the box. The middle box should have a piece of paper with the words "A Secret" taped on one side and on the opposite side of the box tape the words "Our Thoughts." Arrange boxes as shown in illustration.

Lesson

Begin by having the participants think of an unhappy feeling they've experienced recently. This feeling could be anger, sadness, jealousy, resentment, or whatever comes to mind. If the youngsters are old enough to write, have them jot the word that best expresses their unhappy feeling on a piece of paper and put it in the box labeled "Unhappiness."

Next, have them write on another slip of paper the experience or condition that they think made them feel bad. Encourage concise statements such as "friend got invited and I didn't," "fell off my bike," "Dad wouldn't let me watch favorite program," "lost my cat," "Sister scribbled on my homework assignment." These slips go into the box labeled "Experience."

Now point out that between the two boxes there is a box titled "A Secret." This is a very important secret that few people know about. If the youngsters are aware enough, you can asking probing questions as to what must always intercede between an experience and unhappiness. Turn the box around to reveal the "Our Thoughts" label and explain, in your own way, that the experience never creates the unhappiness. This comes from our thoughts about the experience. Another person can have the same experience and not feel the pain, anger, or sadness. Point out that they have a choice to "feel bad" or "feel good," depending on the thoughts they choose to think.

With the help of God they can learn to choose thoughts that bring happiness. Turn the third box to the word "Happiness." Share that the secret is that we can have whichever one we really want, the Happiness or the Unhappiness, by learning to choose Our Thoughts. God can help us do that if we go quietly within and ask.

There may be volunteers who will share their painful experiences. Use these for group exploration as to how a different mode of thinking would lessen the pain. If there are no volunteers, have examples ready that are at their level of understanding. Focus on the positive options.

Just keep in mind that there is always someone somewhere who would not see that experience or condition as a reason to be unhappy. Our thinking creates our happiness.

A guided meditation might be an appropriate way to end the lesson. Have the children ask for God's help in looking at a particular experience or problem in a new way. Allow plenty of time for listening.

I learn something from each experience as I turn to God.

14

My Thoughts
Join All Others

Strainer; large bowl; spoon; package or dish of flour; cinnamon (or instant tea or coffee).

_____Lesson_____

The bowl stands for the thought world—the thought atmosphere that surround us all; the strainer represents our minds, each person's individual mind; the flour and cinnamon are our thoughts.

Elicit a happy or loving thought from one of the youngsters and have him or her put a spoonful of flour representing that thought into the strainer. Give the strainer a shake (a child might enjoy doing this), and watch how these happy thoughts leave the individual mind and spread out into the world of thought—the one Mind. Explain how minds are joined in this thought atmosphere and because of this no one is alone in experiencing the effects of his or her thinking. Everyone feels a little happier because of that joyful thought that just went out.

You might go on to say, "Let's see what would happen if one of you put an unhappy or fearful thought into your mind." Invite a youngster to share such a thought while dropping a spoonful of cinnamon into the strainer. As the strainer is shaken or the thought is stirred around in mind, observe together how it permeates the thought atmosphere just as effectively as the happy thought. Get conclusions from the youngsters that some people might choose to be a bit more unhappy because of that thought.

If the children are old enough, discuss how, because minds are joined, we sometimes tune into others' thoughts and they to ours. They may have examples of when they knew what someone was going to say or do before it was done, or of when others tuned into what they were thinking.

You could extend the conversation to "race consciousness" (concepts accepted by most or all of mankind that limit spiritual realization), and how this can affect us even though we're not aware of it. Examples of collective or race thinking might be offered as spoonsful of flour or cinnamon go into the strainer. The TV, radio, and newspapers are often good sources of group thinking. Be sure to talk about how we can choose our experience. We do not need to be victims of the world's thinking, such as, "Now is the flu season."

Suggested
Affirmation

My thoughts affect the entire world.

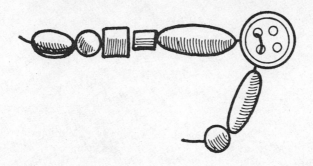

15

We Are All
Connected

Materials

A variety of beads or buttons (with two or four holes, not shanks); a long piece of cord or string. With a group of children you could have individual strings, or each could add beads to one very long string.

Lesson

In this lesson the cord represents Spirit or God; the beads are our individuality or individualization of Spirit; and the colors, shapes, and textures represent our different personalities and appearances.

Have the children choose beads (or buttons) to place on the string and a name that each bead could represent— Dad, Uncle Charlie, Nana, baby sister, teacher, mailman, and so on. Put one on to represent each of them. Each bead or button should have a different feel and look about it, just as does each person.

Lead the children to see that all these people are connected by a common thread at the center of their being. This cord that connects us might be called Spirit, or Life, or God. People have many names for it. Remind them that this cord of Spirit that connects us all is at the center of everyone. Make sure they know you are not talking about the center of the physical body.

It is good to look beyond the beads' various colors and shapes, or beyond people's different appearances and personalities, and to know that way inside, at the center of us, we are all the same. This center of us is perfect and is the most important part of us. If we just look at people as beads of different colors and shapes, we can feel very separate and different from others. But if we choose to remember that we are all connected by the cord of Spirit and Love, we can feel close to others. We can choose to look for this center of perfection within people rather than just looking at the outer person.

If appropriate, you might take a few minutes for them to still their minds and reach for that cord of peace and perfection, the Spirit within.

Suggested Affirmation

I look for the perfection in others.

16

My World Reflects
What I Put into It

A small free-standing mirror; a hand or purse mirror for each child; a felt-tip pen; piece of dark paper and bright paper; teaspoon; paper clip.

Lesson

Have the children play with the mirror and observe how it reflects whatever object it is pointed toward. Point out how accurately it pictures whatever is reflected into it. Explain that there is a spiritual law that works just the same way as the mirror and just as exactly. The mirror represents our world. The world picks up and reflects back to us our states of mind (our moods and thoughts). Another way of saying it is that we live in a world of mirrors, and all we see is us.

The mirror of our world is called effect, and our states of mind are called the **cause** of that effect. With felt-tip pen write EFFECT on your mirror. You might direct the mirror at a spoon, so that the child will see two spoons. Ask which is real, the one on the table or the one in the mirror. Explain that, just as the one in the mirror is only a reflection, all of life is simply a reflection of that which is placed in front of it.

If our minds are full of love and peace and abundance, the mirror of life will reflect that in our world. If our minds are full of fear, doubt, or anger, the mirror of life will image that in our world. An angry person or fearful situation could come into our lives. If we're feeling sorry for ourselves, the mirror (life) will reflect back more experiences to help us feel even sorrier for ourselves.

At any time, we can withdraw an old thought image and place a new one in front of the mirror to bring us more happiness. Use a piece of black or gray paper to indicate a negative thought. Pull that away from the front of the mirror and substitute a new positive thought image (yellow, pink, or orange paper could be used). Suggest some images.

Show what happens if you only half-withdraw the unhappy thoughts and only halfway form new happy ones. Reflect in your mirror half black paper and half colored paper. Explain that one's experiences in life will be the same way—a combination of both the positive and the negative.

Another idea that can be illustrated with the mirror is that it can reflect large images just as easily as it does small images. Place a small item, such as a paper clip, in front of it, and then a larger item, such as a cup. Apply this as you see fit to areas where the children might be needing to think bigger and stop limiting themselves. The mirror, or our world, can reflect big dreams and goals as easily as small ones. If we don't think big, we can't expect big things to come to us. In all things encourage children to think their biggest thoughts, and then to think a little bigger.

Close the lesson by helping the children to see that we each need to put into our minds only the best, the kindest, and most unlimited thoughts, because that is what will be reflected back to us. Affirmations can help us do this.

I look for the good in all things and the best in all people.

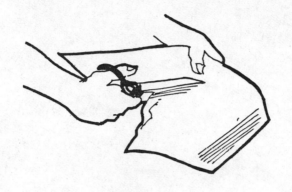

17

The Formative
Power of
Imagination

Scissors and paper for each child.

_____Lesson_____

Point out that the paper represents the energy or substance of which the universe is made. The scissors represent our imagination.

Tell the children that they can use their imaginations (scissors) to cut anything they choose out of the universal substance. It has been said that imagination is the scissors of the mind. With those scissors (their imagination) tell them they can choose whatever they would like to experience in life. Get them to think of specific examples and then cut symbolic shapes out of the paper. Initiate this by stating concrete examples of your own— a trip, a certain job or talent, a new home, and so on. Cut symbols of these from your own paper.

Explain that the imagination is one of the greatest powers we have and should be used with great care. Let them know that whatever they vividly imagine with faith on a repeated basis can come into their lives, so they must imagine only things they want to experience. Give examples of the use of the imagination as it relates to the children's world at this time (winning a prize, making a new friend, illness, failing a test, losing something, falling while skating, and so on). Remind them that they have the choice of using their imaginations either constructively or destructively. Also their imagination "muscles" need to be exercised like any other muscle or it may atrophy from lack of use. If time allows, you may wish to include some creative thinking exercises to further stretch the imagination.

Conclude with a visual imagery exercise in which the children use their imaginations to construct some good they want in their lives. With their eyes closed, get them to image such things as:

- what a perfect day would be like from start to finish.
- where they would most want to go if they could take a trip.
- a school paper or report with an A grade on it.

Suggested Affirmation

I use my imagination creatively and wisely.

18

Faith Forms
What We
Have Faith in

Pre-heated oven; prepared cookie sheets and cookie dough for a cookie that will bake in about ten minutes. There are many such recipes available. If the lesson is done before school, do it early enough for the children to see the cookies come out of the oven and take some to school as a reminder of the lesson. If the second analogy is chosen, have a roll-out cookie dough and cookie cutters.

Lesson

Let the children add the ingredients and help mix the dough if time allows. Discuss how each item is equivalent to thoughts, words, and feelings.

If time is not available for the above, at least let the children drop the cookie dough onto the cookie sheet, explaining that each spoonful is to represent one of their thoughts or words (verbalized thought).

Explain that the oven represents faith—that power that acts upon our words and thoughts. Say "just as the oven has the power to take this cookie dough and turn it into yummy cookies, so faith takes your thoughts and words and turns them into experiences or things that we can see or touch." Faith actually draws from the invisible to the visible. For instance, faith that studying hard will bring an A on the spelling test, or that getting chilled will cause a cold, produces those results.

You may wish to use another analogy and let certain cookie cutters represent the "good" the children have faith in and expect to have happen in their lives. The cookie dough represents the energy or substance of which all things in the universe are made. Allow the children to experience shaping the dough into the "good" they want with appropriately labeled cutters.

Note: This lesson is best used after "The Formative Power of Imagination" (Lesson 17). Our imagination creates ideas of what we want, but it needs to be coupled with the power of faith to take shape in the physical world.

Suggested
Affirmation

With faith in God, I achieve my heart's desire.

19

We Absorb
Our Environment

(This could be divided into two lessons, with each part enlarged upon, if so desired.)

Materials

Part A: A collection of pictures clipped from magazines, calendars, newspapers, and so forth. Have a variety of both negative and positive types, such as beautiful scenes, happy people, nourishing food, war scenes, accidents, drinking, and smoking.

Part B: Two sauce dishes, one with dirty-looking, dark water and one with clean, clear water; two sponges of a size that will fit in the dishes.

Lesson

Spread out the pictures or display them for easy viewing. Explain that there is a law of life that states when we look at a picture of a thing, we are in touch with the spirit of that thing. As we view a picture frequently, we absorb some of the qualities it contains.

Show, one at a time, the positive, beneficial pictures and ask what some of the qualities in them are that the children would like to absorb or experience. Next show the negative pictures and talk about the qualities they contain that would be harmful to absorb.

Expand the conversation to include all the pictures they view frequently in their daily life: TV, movies, pictures on the walls at home and school, magazines, billboards, pictures on buses, and so on. Discuss the effect these might have if they are viewed regularly and their qualities are absorbed.

Explain that all these pictures are a part of their environment or physical surroundings. Point out the two dishes of water, the one representing an environment of negative influences, the other representing an environment that is positive and uplifting. Saying that the sponge is like a person, place one in each dish and watch it absorb its "environment."

Discuss how we, as people, tend to absorb much that goes on around us, which is why those who care about us don't want us in certain settings, around certain people, or watching certain TV shows and movies.

A sponge full of dirty water is going to have no room left for the pure clean water. Some of the dirty water will have to be squeezed out or eliminated to make room for the clean water. Demonstrate. The same is true with us.

For instance, if we have friends that encourage us to do things we know are not right, we may have to eliminate them from our life in order to make room for more beneficial friendships. Or if we spend time watching TV shows that don't contain qualities we really want in our life, we need to eliminate them so we have more time to impress our spongelike minds with qualities or ideas we do desire. Choose examples that your particular child or children can relate to, while emphasizing these two points: we tend to absorb those qualities prevalent in our environment; the negative often has to be eliminated to make room for the positive.

A guided meditation might follow in which children

get in touch with what would be beneficial to add to or
eliminate from their environment.

Suggested
_____Affirmation_____

*I release what is not for my best and choose a positive,
uplifting environment.*

20

Change Is Needed
for Growth

(This lesson would be most useful when a child is at a place in life where some change is needed, where a risk needs to be taken. This could be something like joining Scouts or a soccer team, going away to camp, staying overnight with a friend for the first time, entering a new school, or whatever feels like a risk to that child.)

Materials

A tiny clay flower pot or the smallest sized cardboard transplanting pot; a tangled mass of string stuffed into the pot, and an artificial flower inserted into the string mass. (A real houseplant that has gotten rootbound and needs transplanting would make the best illustration.)

Lesson

Point out the mass of string, explaining that this represents the roots of the flower. Say that roots need a lot of soil to grow in, but these have grown so that there is hardly room for soil in the pot. At this point one needs to remove the plant from the old pot and put it into a larger one, or the plant will always be limited in size. Explain that people are just like that flower, and at times we, too, need more room to grow.

Compare the pot to the children's old ways of thinking about themselves. The old pot, or ways, can be so comfortable that sometimes we need to push ourselves out of this "comfort zone." If not, our growth would be stunted just as the growth of a plant is stunted when it's in a container too small for it. The old pot met the needs of the plant at one time and was good for the plant. Now that the plant has grown, a change is necessary to enable the plant to continue its growth.

Discuss how, in order to grow and become all that they can be, they must change their old ideas about themselves. Help them see change as a means of "becoming." An acorn breaking apart to sprout the new tree, or an egg becoming a chicken are excellent examples for this concept.

Suggested
_____Affirmation_____

I welcome change in my life because it helps me grow into greater happiness.

21

There Is
No Separation

Materials

A silver or stainless steel teaspoon.

Lesson

Compare the teaspoon to us, and the metal that was used to make the spoon to God (or Spirit).

You might explain it this way: "If we were to take all the silver (or steel) out of this spoon, there would no longer be a spoon. There is no way we can separate the silver from the spoon and still have the spoon.

"Now let's say that this spoon is like you and the silver in it is like God or Spirit. There is no way you can be separated from God because God is in you just as the silver is in the spoon. God is a special love energy that is in everybody and everything. Nothing is separate from God.

Explain, at the children's level of understanding, that the attributes of God are within them: love, peace, order, wisdom, understanding, and so forth. They can call upon these powers to activate them in their own lives. Even though these qualities are in them, they need to be affirmed or called forth. Use a particular example, depending upon the needs of the children. For instance, if order is a need in their lives, they can know that they have this in them because it is an attribute of God, and God is in them. They can remind themselves of the order within by saying, "I am one with divine order."

You might suggest that they play a little mind game, and every time they see a teaspoon they think about God being in them just like the silver is in the spoon. Have them go on to silently affirm a God characteristic such as, "I am one with the love of God."

Suggested
Affirmation

I am one with God.

22

Take Time
To Relax

_____Materials_____

One average-sized rubber band; a box or book that the rubber band will barely stretch around.

_____Lesson_____

Pull the rubber band to show how much stretch there is in it, and then put it around the large box or book. Talk to the youngsters about what might happen if it were stretched out that much for very long. Tell them that, if a rubber band is kept under tension (stretched out all the time), it will deteriorate rapidly and break. We must allow it to return to its natural state (remove from box) in order for it to last a long time.

Discuss how people are very much like the rubber band. They also need to relax or they won't function as well as they are designed to. There's an adage that says when things get tight, something's got to give. When people are under tension or strain, two areas that often give way are their health or their relationships. The youngsters may have other examples, such as school work, piano practice, and so forth.

Someone once said that real maturity is not growing up so much as growing in. Explain to the children that they have much inside them that is worth sharing with other people. If they take some time to relax and listen within each day, they can bring it out. This is the source of creative ideas if they wish to become more original. You might discuss what time of day would be best for them to get alone and relax with closed eyes for a few minutes.

Give each child a pretty colored rubber band as a reminder to take time to be quiet and listen each day.

This lesson could be especially valuable for overly active children. Also, it could be slanted toward a better understanding of the need for quiet time for the adults in their lives.

You may wish to take an extra few minutes and have the children do a relaxation exercise at this time. The simplest is to have them close their eyes, take three or four really deep breaths, and then think about a happy experience. Another simple but effective technique is to have them get in a very relaxed position, close their eyes, and hum a single note on each out-breath. There are a number of books available now with centering or meditation exericses for children.

Suggested Affirmation

I take time each day to relax and listen within.

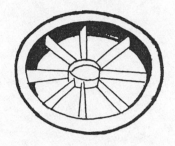 

23

Our Connection
with God
and Each Other

Apple cutter. If this is not available, a picture or sketch of a bicycle wheel will do nicely. (An apple is not needed for the lesson.)

_____Lesson_____

The wheel shape, as illustrated by the apple cutter, graphically shows our connection with each other and with God.

The hub of the wheel or center of the apple slicer represents God, or whatever term you use for the Almighty. We, the people, are the spokes. As can be seen, the closer we get to God-awareness, the closer we get to each other. This works the other way around too, because as we get closer to each other we get closer to God.

When we're feeling really loving toward someone we are kind, generous, and thoughtful. We are expressing Godlike qualities. When we are angry and hateful toward another, we put ourselves farther away from an understanding of God. We can readily see (point to outside edge of cutter) that the farther away we are from another, the farther we are from God awareness.

Elicit examples of how people separate themselves

from each other. You might wish to explain that that is why to forgive anybody whom you could possibly have bad feelings toward is advised as the first step of prayer. Such feelings separate you from others and, therefore, from God-consciousness, which is total, unconditional love. It has been said that the only problem there is, is separation.

The more we work to express all the qualities that are Godlike (peace, love, harmony, order), the closer we'll feel to other people. Other people will feel this and want to be closer to us. Together we move closer to complete God awareness. Encourage a discussion here of the ways that we can express Godlike qualities in our everyday lives. Start with a personal and specific example.

Suggested
Affirmation

The closer I grow to people, the closer I feel to God.

24

You Can't Give Love
Unless You Have Love

Materials

Turkey baster; bowl of water; empty bowl.

Lesson

The turkey baster represents the children and you. The water represents perfect love, which is unconditional acceptance and the absence of all negative emotions. In order to be filled with perfect love, we need to first empty ourselves of all feelings or emotions that keep us from accepting love. We cannot fully accept love when we feel unworthy or undeserving. Some of the emotions that make us feel undeserving are guilt, anger, jealousy, and resentment. These can fill us up and keep perfect love out of our awareness. Discuss such emotions and low self-esteem at the children's level of understanding. They know what makes them feel unworthy of an abundance of love. Explain that these are all up in the top of the baster, and have the child squeeze the bulb hard to eliminate this negativity. Holding it squeezed, guide the baster into the bowel of water (perfect love). Observe that, as the hand is released, love fills the baster up. Let the children experiment to see that, if the negativity hadn't been squeezed out, love (the water) wouldn't come in.

If the children are old enough, you can take the lesson the next step and teach that one can only love others as much as one loves oneself. It is love of self that can motivate us to clean out the bulb of negativity. The empty bowl represents "all others." With the baster full of love, have them share this with others by emptying the baster into the bowl. How much they have to share depends on how full they (baster) are with love.

Affirmations are a great way to replace negative thought patterns with positive ones and to build self-esteem. Help the children create some to suit their needs.

Suggested Affirmation

I am filled with love for myself and others.

25

Choose
Your Thoughts

Materials

Put out several typical kitchen items from which a parent must make choices, such as:

2 packages or cans of soup
2 sizes of pans and rice package
a pudding box and a jello box
a grocery ad
2 or 3 similar recipes

Lesson

Point out to the children that these items represent some of the constant choices you have to make in the kitchen: which recipe is best, which soup for dinner, which size pan for the package of rice, which is the best buy at the store, and so on. Demonstrate some right choices with these materials, such as the recipe that would be most suitable.

Share how we are continually making choices throughout our day, though we may not be aware of them. We are constantly choosing thoughts and feelings. We're reaching out with loving thoughts or withdrawing because of fear. The one brings us joy, the other pain. All day long we have the opportunity to choose the thoughts that can either hurt or help us. When we're feeling anger, hurt, or other unhappy feelings, we can remind ourselves that it is really fear underneath.

The law of attraction says we attract that which we think about, so we want to be sure that we choose love thoughts, not fear thoughts. Love thoughts are healing and helpful, and they certainly bring more happiness into our lives.

If the children are old enough, teach that fear can arrive when there is a false belief in power other than God. Since there is only one Power, God the good, there is nothing to fear.

Throughout the day we adults need to keep asking ourselves if we are acting out of love or fear. Remember that more is caught than taught. We teach what we are.

Suggested Affirmation

I let go of fear and choose only loving thoughts.

26

Listening
for Guidance

Large bowl of water; wooden spoon (or any large spoon); picture of something reflected in water (optional). Or, if possible, take the children to a lake or pond.

_____Lesson_____

Begin by discussing how it is possible to look into a quiet pool and see the reflection of a tree growing on its bank. If the water is rough or churning we lose the image. Encourage the children to remember such a scene as you discuss the lesson.

Pretend that the bowl is the pool and the spoon (held vertically) is the tree. As you swish the water, explain that if the wind were blowing the water, or children were splashing in it, one would be unable to see the tree's reflection. Go on to explain, at the level of their understanding, that we each have a guidance factor within us. Some call it the Inner Knower, and others call it such names as Higher Self or Holy Spirit. It tries to speak to us and give us direction, but it can be heard only if our minds are calm and still, like a very quiet pool. The beauty of the tree is not seen in churning water, and the guidance of Spirit is not heard by a churning mind. An overly busy mind gives rise to problems. But when the mind is made very quiet, these problems are usually answered. A quiet mind can see beyond confusion to a solution.

Suggest they practice many times a day stilling their minds so as to be able to listen to the still small voice of Spirit. You may wish to suggest specific meditation techniques, such as holding a word in mind like Peace or Love, staring at an object, or making a steady humming sound. There are many, many more.

As is possible with many of the lessons, role-playing could enhance the teaching. One child could whisper a message, such as, "Call home right away," while another child is busy with noisy thoughts (churning the water) and not able to hear it.

Suggested Affirmation

I still my mind and listen within for guidance.

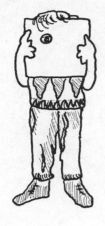

27

Judge Not

This lesson can be divided into two parts if desired.

Materials

Part A: Have for each child a small portion of a picture from a magazine, calendar, or advertisement flyer. For instance, if the picture is of a face, cut out just the mouth; if it's a nature scene, cut out just a tree or a bit of the lake.

Part B: A sheet of typing paper for each child with a small hole punched in the middle. The children can punch it themselves with a pencil or it can be prepunched.

Lesson

Hand each child the piece of picture mentioned above and ask them to give an opinion about the whole picture. They'll find this task to be no more than a guessing game. They will see that they just don't have enough facts to make an accurate judgment. Explain that this is true about most of the judgments we make in this world, especially those regarding people.

Hold up a picture of an ear or nose and say something like, "Just as we can't tell much about this face from this small bit of information, we really can't tell much about a person from just appearance or actions. In order to judge anyone rightly we would have to be aware of such a wide range of things from his past and present that fair judgment would be impossible." Remind them that all we see are bits of anything—never the whole picture—so we need to give up thinking we understand the whole from the bits. This is wisdom. Wisdom is not judgment.

Next hand each child the typing paper and have them punch a small hole in the center to peek through. Ask them to look through it at you and tell how much of the room they can see. Encourage them to look around the room, noting how their vision is limited by the parameter of the hole. Help them be aware that they can only see what is directly in front of them.

Go on to discuss how most of us are only looking at the world through peepholes. Our vision of other people is a peephole vision. You might have them get close and look at each other through their peepholes. Make the point that, just as they were able to see only a fragment of each other through the hole, that is all they're really seeing or understanding of anyone or any situation. Our awareness at this level of development is very limited. Some people say we're asleep. Therefore, we need to be so careful we're not judging people or situations. We just don't see the whole picture. We don't have sufficient awareness.

There is only One that has that much awareness. There is only One whose judgment is perfect. Only by staying open-minded will we be able to hear His guidance, His wisdom. When our mind is made up, it is impossible to hear Spirit within us. We can ask for wisdom in any situation and then we can go into the silence and listen for God's guidance. The lesson might close with a silent meditation preceded by guided deep breathing for relaxation.

I let go of all judgment and rely on the wisdom of God.

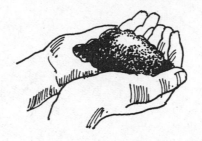

28

Things Take Form
According to
Our Thought

Materials

Baker's "clay" is suggested, but you may wish to use bread dough, cookie dough, play dough, or natural clay. Give each child a chunk about the size of a small grapefruit.

Recipe:
4 c. flour
1 c. salt
1½ c. water

Mix ingredients and knead with hands for about five minutes. This inedible dough is popular for Christmas tree ornaments, jewelry, and figurines. Objects can be dried at room temperature or baked on a cookie sheet in a 350 degree oven for about 40–60 minutes. They are done when light brown or when a toothpick inserted in the thickest part comes out clean, showing that the dough has hardened.

Lesson

Let the children play with the dough in their own way for a bit, and then suggest that it could symbolize the substance or energy of which all things are made. Since thought molds substance into form, suggest that they think of their hands as thoughts. You might even print thoughts on their hands with a water-soluble felt marker. Have them squeeze, poke, and pull at the dough while thinking, "My thoughts are molding this substance." Tell them that this is how thoughts become things.

Next, have them form the dough into some actual things as a reminder of the lesson. Sometimes the things we would like to give form to are not easy to make with our hands, so we use symbols. "What could we make to symbolize happiness or love?" "What are some of the thoughts you want to mold into form?"

If they choose to make ornaments that are to be hung, a paper clip should be inserted in the top before drying or baking. Completed objects can be kept natural or decorated with felt-tip pens, enamel, water colors, food dye, or half tempera and half white glue.

Suggested
Affirmation

I watch my thoughts because thoughts become things.

29

Thoughts Are Gifts

Small box wrapped like a gift.

Begin by explaining that the little gift box doesn't really have a gift in it, but is a symbol of many gifts we receive each day. Your dialogue might run something like this:

"For something to be a gift it does not have to be put in a box and have a ribbon around it. It does not have to be something that is bought. What are some of the gifts you like to receive that are not bought or wrapped?" Offer ideas such as a warm smile, a special favor, help when stuck or in a hurry, a hug or pat on the back, an invitation, a word of praise or appreciation, a promise to be taken somewhere special, a listening ear when we have a problem, prayers or loving thoughts sent our way.

"Do you see that you receive more gifts each day than you were aware of? How many do you think you receive each day? Well, I have a big surprise for you. In truth, you are receiving thousands and thousands of gifts each day. You do not consciously know about these gifts, but one part of your mind knows. How is this possible?"

You might continue the dialogue with: "There is only

one Mind on which each person draws, and we're all part of that one Mind. That is why we say that all mankind are brothers and sisters. Because there is only one Mind and one Spirit, you are truly connected at some level with everyone on the planet. Each day thousands of people are giving gifts to each other, and these gifts are blessing everyone. The more thoughts and acts of joy and happiness in the world, the more joy you'll feel because of your connection with everyone else."

Elaborate on the unity of mankind at the child's level of awareness. If time allows, you may wish to include a meditation, visualizing all the world's people joyfully giving gifts of various types.

You may want to expand the lesson by stating that they in turn are giving gifts to brothers and sisters around the world when they befriend or help others or think loving thoughts. Each time they give any sort of gift they are blessing multitudes of others. The children could write "thought gifts" they would like to send out on slips of paper and place them in the box. These can be reread or added to when they have a special need. As with many of the lessons, this lesson can be effectively offered via one or two puppets.

Suggested
Affirmation

Today I rejoice because of the many gifts I give and receive.

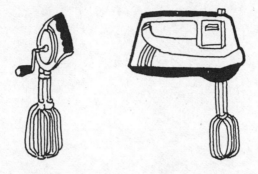

30

The Hard Way
Versus the Easy Way

Hand eggbeater and an electric beater.

Demonstrate to the children how both of these tools do pretty much the same thing, but with one it's a lot harder work. Allow the children to try out both. You might whip up some soap flakes in water, or partially set gelatin dessert, or whipping cream. Lead them to see how much easier, with its various speeds, the electric beater is for whipping.

Explain that using the hand beater for a very long time can be exhausting. It is harder because it is detached from power, whereas the electric beater is easy because it is attached to power. Point out the cord and outlet as the channel for the electrical power.

Discuss how the same is true with people. We have a choice of using the higher power, God power, or of not using it and going it alone. The latter way creates exhaustion and unsatisfactory results. When we ask for the help of the One Power, we are tapping into the source of all love, wisdom, and knowledge. We can receive guidance that is just right for our own particular project, and the energy to see it through.

If we know that there is a higher power, a spiritual power, that we can use, but we choose not to, it's just like knowing how to read and not reading. It's like having the instruction manual for a piece of equipment but trying to figure it out without reading the instructions. Would you rather make toast with a toaster or a candle?

Through prayer or meditation you can tune into the higher power, the One Mind. Simply ask for help or guidance and then quiet your mind and listen for what you are to do next. End the lesson with a short listening meditation.

Suggested Affirmation

I turn to a higher power.

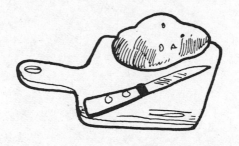

31

Cut Your
Problem in Half

Potato or lump of clay; small cutting board; knife.

_____Lesson_____

It has been said that welcoming problems without resentment cuts the problem in half, and this is the focus of the lesson.

Life is God's schoolhouse, full of wonderful lessons to be learned from the problems we encounter. Our attitudes toward these problems are part of our lesson. Our attitudes can make learning fun or not fun.

Explain that the potato or chunk of clay represents a problem, any kind of problem the children might meet in life. Disclose that you know of a way to make that problem smaller, a way to cut it down to half its size. You might first ask for some ideas from the children. They may have great thoughts for making problems or challenges seem smaller. Share that one secret to cutting a problem in half is to cut or remove the resentment from it.

Demonstrate by cutting the vegetable in half. Label the removed part Resentment, and show that that is what made the problem seem twice its size. When we let go of those feelings of annoyance and bless the problem, not only will it seem smaller, but we will have freed up energy to use in looking for solutions. Resentment, like all negative emotions, is a form of fear and, consequently, drains energy.

Help the children see that when they learn to welcome their problems as interesting challenges, as opportunities for learning, as simply the lessons that life is giving them, all their problems will seem half the size.

Remind them that they never need to be alone in dealing with a problem or with resentment. God is always with us and can be asked for help. The spirit of God in us can turn resentment into love.

Note: This lesson has been successfully done with puppets. Use your imagination.

Suggested
Affirmation

I accept my problems as exciting challenges and turn resentful feelings over to God.

32

There Is a Gift
in Every Problem

Materials

Several sheets of scratch paper and a pencil; a small wastebasket about ½ full of crumpled newspaper; a tiny gift box (with bow on it) under the newspaper. Inside the gift box have slips of paper with messages at the children's level of understanding. Here are suggestions:

- My problems help me to grow.
- Problems are friends because they help me become strong.
- There is a lesson in this challenge, and we are never presented with lessons until we are ready to learn from them.
- Within every disadvantage there is an advantage. I look for it now.
- Something good will come from this problem.
- My problems are learning opportunities.
- There are no bad experiences.
- What's the gift from this experience?

Ask the children to name some of the problems in their lives right now. As each is named, write it on a piece of scratch paper and invite the children to crumple it and toss it in the wastebasket. Older children may write down their own problems. Suggest that they include anxieties about future problems that may be of real concern. Have them do the same with some local, national, and international problems.

Explain that there is always a gift hidden within any problem or misfortune they may ever have, but they need to look for it. Hand the wastebasket to a child and ask him or her to look within the midst of those problems for the gift hidden there.

Have the child open the box and together read the slips of paper inside. Encourage discussion of these concepts, and be prepared with some examples from your own experience to illustrate them.

Suggest that in finding the gift in a problem it is helpful to rename the problem. Call problems "challenges" or "learning opportunities."

The children might like to have similar gift boxes in their rooms as reminders of the lesson.

Suggested Affirmation

There is good for me in every situation.

(You may prefer one from the list at the beginning of this lesson.)

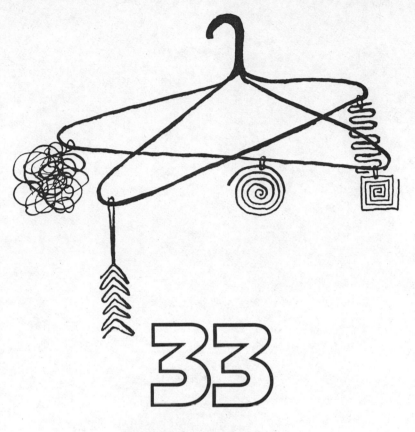

33

Rise Above
the Problem

Materials

Yarn or string. If demonstrating, have eight pieces about two or three feet in length. If it is to be a "hands on" experience for the youngsters, have similar lengths for each of them. Optional materials for mobile project: waxed paper, liquid starch for dipping the yarn, two wire coat hangers per child.

Lesson

It has been well stated that we should not try to solve a problem at the level of a problem. We need to rise above the problem and see it as God sees it, which is not at all. Our problems are best solved from a spiritual perspective, not by mental power.

Begin with one length of yarn and thoroughly knot and tangle it. If the youngsters are participating, invite them to do the same with theirs. Tangle and knot it so well that it would be most difficult to unravel.

You can then explain that this mess represents our individual human problems, the messes that we find ourselves in sometime or other. Mentally we might wrestle with this problem and try to untangle it, but usually this mental approach is long, frustrating, difficult, and not too effective. Ask how easy they think it would be to untangle and unknot that piece of yarn. Explain that it would be like trying to solve a problem all by themselves. They might miss a knot here and there and so come up with a solution that is not the very best.

If they turn the problem over to the Higher Power—to God, it will be solved in the very best way possible. God rises above the mess and doesn't get caught up in it. In fact, God does not see our problems but only our perfection.

Let's say this tangled mess represents a relationship problem. Somebody is difficult to get along with. They're always giving us a bad time. Where we see disharmony, God sees only harmony. This is how God would see that relationship. (Take another strand of yarn and make a harmonious design. Invite the youngsters to do the same, if participating).

If we can learn to see as God sees and see all of our relationships as loving and harmonious, we would not have a tangled mess like the knotted yarn in our life. (Toss the tangled yarn aside.)

Now let's make another knotty problem. (Knot another piece of yarn and tangle it.) This is a health problem we're having or someone we know is having. But we must remember that God sees us all as whole and healthy like this. (Shape another piece of yarn and invite the youngsters to do the same.) The more we can raise ourselves above the thoughts of illness and see ourselves and others as God sees us, the more healthy we'll all be.

Let's say we are experiencing disorder and confusion in our life. (Tangle another piece of yarn.) By rising above the problem and seeing it from the spiritual viewpoint, we would see that only Divine Order exists. (Make a pleasing orderly shape.) As we choose to see perfect order we would draw that to us.

Or maybe we're seeing ourselves so very limited in our abilities so as not to be able to do things as well as other people. Again, we need to get way above that man-made problem and see ourselves as God does, as having unlimited ability because of the Spirit within us. (Again shape a strand of yarn in an orderly design.)

Suggest that the next time they have a problem, instead of using human effort, they ask God, the One Mind that knows all, to work out the perfect solution. God always works things out in the way that is best for us and for everybody else too. This can bring about astounding results beyond what those our human minds can imagine or accomplish, but we must sincerely *ask*.

Stress that after they have asked, they need to take time to listen to the Spirit of God within us so that they will know what their part is in the solution. Follow-up action based on any guidance or impression they get should also be stressed. Spirit works through us. Prayer plus action is the formula.

Note: As a reminder of this lesson, consider making a mobile. The lengths of yarn can be dipped in starch and shaped on waxed paper. Make some shapes into the tangled messes to represent problems and make designs to represent the way God sees us—healthy, orderly, harmonious, talented, and so forth. After drying overnight, remove the shapes from the waxed paper and hang from coat hangers or bent wires to form mobiles.

Suggested
Affirmation

I turn my problems over to God and do what I am guided to do.

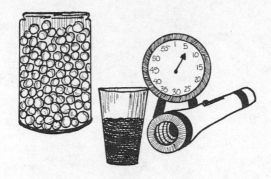

34

Using Our
Daily Energy

Materials

Glass jar, about pint size; enough large marbles to fill it; glass of muddy-colored water; flashlight. If marbles are not available, try walnuts in the shell, or stones. Optional: A timer such as used is in the kitchen.

Lesson

Begin by explaining that the jar represents the body, their's or anybody's. Within the body are many atoms. Add the marbles saying that these represent the atoms that make up the cells of the body. You might mention that they are very far apart in the body, but because they are constantly moving they make our body look and feel solid. There's really a lot of empty space in the body or in any material object. Point to a table, chair, book, and so forth.

Next take the flashlight and shine light down over the jar (the body), while stating that the light represents the daily portion of energy received each day from God. Explain that we make constant choices, minute by minute, as to how we use that energy. Whenever we think unhappy or unloving thoughts, the energy we have received from God is colored or qualified by that thinking.

When we think as God would have us think—positively, constructively, unlimited—our energy is permeated or colored with that feeling. That energy, being God-like, is attracted back to our God-Self and deposited in our spiritual bank account. We can draw on it when extra energy is needed in our life for a special purpose.

But what of the energy that is not God-like? The negativity has made it dark and heavy so it can't be attracted back to God. Let's say that this glass of muddy-looking water is the light or energy we have misused. We might have used it for anger, hate, criticism, jealousy, worry, self-pity, or selfishness. The children may be able to give some specific examples of the ways they have misused their energy.

Pour the water into the jar, explaining that since it is too impure to be returned to God, it just goes into all the empty spaces in the body. This can make us feel heavy and dense because normally there is light between all these atoms. Shine the flashlight on the marbles again, commenting that our negative thoughts and feelings cut out a lot of the light. Older children might have examples of days when they've felt heavy and days when they've felt light.

Too much misused energy stored in our body can lead to disease, so we need to become very aware of our thoughts and feelings and quickly change the negative ones. One way of doing this is to use a kitchen timer that rings. Carry it around the house and continually set it for every ten to twenty minutes. Each time it rings, check your thinking and feeling to see how your daily gift of energy is being used. Is it being colored by negative feelings and thoughts? Is it pure, positive, and loving enough to be returned to the God-Self (via Law of Attraction)? Self-mastery is how much energy we're able to use positively.

If the question comes up about getting rid of the

muddy-looking stuff around the marbles, suggest that they ask God for forgiveness for the mistaken use of their daily energy. It's important that they also forgive themselves.

In addition, they can start visualizing clear white light beaming through every part of their organism. This can be done as a guided visualization exercise to end the lesson. Also, a timer can go off and they can be asked to check into their thoughts and their feeling state.

Suggested Affirmation

I think, feel, see, hear, and speak only loving thoughts.

35

Watch
Your Words

Bowl of water; salt shaker or small dish of salt; teaspoon.

_____Lesson_____

This lesson shows that words once spoken cannot be taken back, at least not on the physical plane. We can reverse their effect, however, through prayer and positive action.

Tell the youngsters that the small dish or salt shaker represents us, the salt is our words, and the bowl of water is the other person. Shake the salt into the water and observe how the words have dissolved into the other person (if accepted). Personalize the demonstration by telling how you had an argument with someone once and called him names you were sorry about afterward. As you sprinkle salt over the water, explain, "These are the words I used—stupid, lazy, liar, crazy, loser. Afterward, I wanted to take these words back because I didn't really mean them. But do you think I could? Could you get some of those words or salt grains out of the water for me?"

Explain that both our words and thoughts go out into the ocean of thought around us and, just like the salt, can never be retrieved. Therefore, it is so important to think carefully about what we say. Before speaking we can ask ourselves if it would help the thought atmosphere or pollute it. Would it create joy or pain for the other person? Explain how the same is true of thoughts as well as words.

We can help neutralize negative thoughts by substituting in our minds positive, constructive affirmations. We can withdraw a thought of someone as a "loser" by thinking of him as a "winner." Ask how we might lessen the saltiness (negativity) in our bowl of water? Will this work with the thought atmosphere? Positive declarations can dilute a lot of negativity.

Here is a good place to explain to children that all our mistakes can be corrected on the spiritual level by Holy Spirit. It is so important that children are not left with a sense of guilt. Teach that through prayer we can heal past errors and feel forgiven.

Suggested Affirmation

I carefully monitor my words and thoughts.

36

The Aspects of Mind

Kitchen funnel. Put a strip of non-transparent tape around the funnel just above the stem, as shown in the diagram. As an alternative, heavy paper could be shaped to represent the cone of a funnel, and a paper tube insert could form the stem.

Lesson

The aspects of mind discussed in this lesson are the conscious, the subconscious, and the superconscious.

Lead the discussion along these lines, adapting to the youngsters' level of understanding: "This funnel represents you and me. We'll call it a symbol. This small stem is our bodies. This large cone area represents our minds. The mind has two aspects or parts—the conscious mind, which you are well aware of, and the subconscious part, of which most people are unaware. These aspects of mind make up what we experience as our personalities. (This is our consciousness and it's sometimes referred to as the soul.)

"The narrow strip of tape next to the body or stem represents the conscious mind—the part of the mind you think with. It senses, reasons, evaluates, and chooses.

Because it can make choices, it is known as the decision-maker. Because it has the power to make decisions, it is the ruler of our physical lives.

"The rest of the mind, the much larger portion, is the powerful subconscious. It is exciting to know about because it does so many wonderful things for us. It builds, repairs, and operates the body. It is in charge of all the body processes, such as heartbeat, blood circulation, digestion, and elimination. It is the storehouse of memory and the seat of emotion, habit, and instinct. There are some things it does not do. It cannot think, reason, judge, or reject like our conscious mind does. Since the subconscious cannot do these things, it is under the control of the conscious mind. It can be compared to a computer, which is under the control of the computer programmer, the person who puts information into the computer." For younger children, consider the analogy of a gardener planting seeds in the soil, which is comparable to the subconscious mind. "The soil accepts all seeds from the gardener, just as the subconscious accepts all suggestions or directions from the conscious mind. Now here's the good news: This phase of the mind has the ability to form. It can take any direction or belief our conscious minds give it and give it form."

(*Note:* Here would be a good place to offer some examples from your own experience. Think of times when you instructed the subconscious and, being the malleable substance it is, it formed according to your belief. Offering both negative and positive examples of your having spoken your word or having held a belief and seen it come into existence. You might want to suggest a simple experiment the children can test this on. A popular one is waking and getting up so many minutes earlier than usual without benefit of alarm. Have them set their mental alarm fifteen minutes earlier tomorrow morning by stating as they go to sleep that they will be wide awake and eager to hop out of bed at that time. If the children's understanding level allows, go on to explain about the superconscious Mind.)

Looking back to the funnel, explain that the ability of the subconscious to form is unlimited because it opens up, as can be seen, to the great sea of mind, the formless stuff around us. This is the superconscious or universal Mind that knows everything and can answer our questions if we get quiet and really listen. We always have the choice between letting the limited conscious mind direct our computer mind or inviting in the unlimited, all-knowing power of the superconscious that is just waiting to respond to us. We do the latter by first asking and then quieting our conscious minds and listening within. It can guide us much more accurately than the limited thinking and reasoning ability of our conscious minds. This is why some people meditate or have a "listening time" every day.

There are many affirmations that can relate to this lesson, thus enabling the children to take more control of the directing ability of the conscious mind and to listen within to the superconscious.

Suggested
Affirmation

I think only of good things that I want to happen.

(Remind them that the subconscious will accept their habitual thoughts and give them form.)

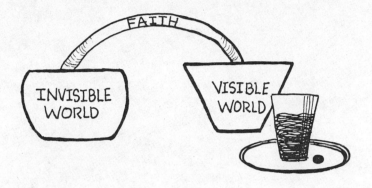

37

Belief
Activates Faith

(This lesson has two analogies and could, therefore, be divided into two lessons.)

Two bowls or glasses; piece of fish-tank hose or bent straw with an end placed in each glass or bowl; glass of water; an antacid seltzer tablet (for instance, Alka Seltzer); labels.

_____Lesson_____

Faith is a God-given power that we all have. It's a continuous rhythmic energy or vibration in the soul of every person. Faith is the power most directly involved in making the invisible visible.

Label one bowl or glass "Invisible World" and another one "Visible World." Explain that everything in the visible world has come forth from the invisible world. There is an energy or substance in the invisible world out of which everything in our world has been formed.

Place the hose or straw between the two vessels and label it Faith. Tell them that it is Faith that draws our good from the invisible to the visible. It is the power that says "yes" to what has not been seen. It says "yes" to God, the one power—the power that can produce our good.

Further explain that this power of Faith is in all of us, but some people activate it and some don't. That's why it appears as though some people have Faith and some don't. Unless our Faith is activated or stimulated, it cannot draw forth our good from the invisible.

Continue by saying, "Belief is what activates Faith and this tablet (seltzer) represents Belief. Let's make a new analogy and say that the water in this glass is Faith. That mighty power is just lying dormant—asleep—inactive. It needs to be awakened or stimulated by our Belief—our conviction."

Drop a tablet into the glass of water and watch how alive and active Faith becomes. The tablet will cause the water to bubble or effervesce.

Note: You may wish to offer an alternative analogy whereby Belief is compared to initiating a siphoning action with the hose. The children could actually watch the water (substance) flow from the Invisible World container into the Visible World container via the hose of Faith. Note that nothing happened until the flow was activated (by Belief). Otherwise, the water (substance) would just be sitting there. To start the siphoning process submerge the hose in the Invisible World vessel that you have filled with water (substance). Cap one end with a finger and lift the hose out, placing it into the Visible World container, which needs to be on a lower level.

Our Belief will draw to us whatever we believe in, but Faith does not draw negatives. It relates only to God and our good. Belief, without Faith in God, can draw anything to us, good or bad. Share with the children that when we draw something harmful or unpleasant to us we have a Belief in it, but not Faith in it.

Affirmative statements can help build our Belief system and strengthen our Faith. With the children, create simple declarations affirming belief in God, belief in peace, belief in supply, belief in healing, belief in good. Nothing can happen unless we expect it. Have them exercise their faith by looking toward the Invisible World, not the Visible World—toward cause, not effect. Offer some examples that would apply to the children's daily world.

**Suggested
Affirmation**

I have faith in God; I have faith in Good.

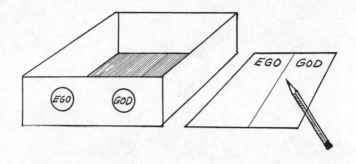

38

Tuning into God

For each child have a box about shoe-box size, a paper that will fit neatly in the bottom of the box, pencil, and crayon. Make two circles out of heavy cardboard for each box and have a paper fastener (brad) through the center of each. These will be radio knobs or dials. Nuts and bolts will work in lieu of paper fasteners.

Lesson

Tell the youngsters that they're going to create a make-believe radio to help them listen to the Voice for God or Holy Spirit. (Let's assume they're old enough to know they won't hear a voice like on the real radio.) Discuss how there are always two voices inside them, two parts of their mind, that are vying for attention. One is the ego, sometimes called the "little self," and it always tries to speak up first. It gets so loud we sometimes can't hear the other voice. Suggest that they take one of the circles or radio knobs and write EGO on it in big letters.

Say that the other voice that tries to speak to us is Holy Spirit (the Voice for God). Suggest that they print GOD on the other circle in nice big letters. Hand each a box for their pretend radio. Say that this is a radio they're going to look inside of so they need to have the open side at the top. Using an ice pick if needed, help each to attach the two knobs to his or her "radio."

Mention how radios often have both an AM and FM dial. If a dial is tuned into an AM station that is all one can hear. One can't hear an FM station unless one turns off the AM station and switches on FM. If we are listening to our ego or "little self" that is all we hear unless we're willing to turn that station off and turn on the station called God. One can't listen to both stations at the same time, just as one can't hear AM and FM at the same time. We get to choose what to listen to: God has given us free will.

If the youngsters are older, you might ask how they can tell whether it's an AM or FM station that is playing. This can lead into a discussion as to how they can tell when it's their "little self" or their "higher self" that is speaking.

Have them take a piece of paper that will fit flat inside their "radio" and draw a line down the middle. On the side where the God dial would be, ask them to write "God Station" as the heading and on the other side "Ego Station." Underneath each heading is to be a list of "clue words" that will show them to which station they're listening.

Proceed with a discussion to bring out such clues. It may come out that there is a feeling of separation from others when ego is speaking, but a feeling of unity or oneness when tuned into God. In that case, they would put the word "separation" in the ego column and the word "unity" in the God column. It may be brought out that there is a feeling of certainty when listening to Spirit and much uncertainty, doubt, and confusion when hearing ego. Again, have them put the key words in the appropriate column. With God there is a feeling of joy, and peace, and love. With ego one may feel fearful, upset, or have attack thoughts. Actually, any fear comes from ego, not God. Someone may comment on the calmness felt when listening to God and the frantic feeling when tuned into ego.

Clue words and phrases should go in each column, but be sure they are at the child's vocabulary level, or they won't serve their purpose as reminders.

You might bring out that ego tends to question and analyze, whereas acceptance accompanies listening to God. Another clue might be the guilt feelings that accompany ego versus the feeling of forgiveness of self and others when tuned into God. As to problems, ego relieves them but doesn't cure them, whereas Holy Spirit cures them completely. Spirit brings a practical solution, one in which everyone involved wins. Ego's purpose is to make conflict. The children may be aware that the ego station is loud, but the God station is usually very soft unless one is a most willing listener. Add further clues to the lists as you or the youngsters think of them.

An appropriate ending for the session would be tuning into God via a listening meditation. This can be a nonspecific meditation just to quiet the mind or it might be for a specific purpose that concerns either the individual or the whole group.

It is hoped that the children would put their shoe-box radios in their bedrooms and look frequently at the lists to see what station is on. They could turn on a kitchen timer or parking-meter timer throughout the day and when it rings they could check to see if they had been listening to God or to ego.

Suggested Affirmation

I choose to listen to the Voice of God and I am guided in all I do.

39

Our Cup of Belief

An assortment of cups, glasses, and containers ranging in size from a thimble to a bucket; pencils and slips of paper.

_____Lesson_____

(Consider using this after the lesson "Belief Activates Faith.")

Our belief is the cup we hold up for Spirit to fill with our good. Our good comes from invisible substance and it is our belief that determines how much we will receive. "As thou hast believed so be it done unto thee." Matthew 8:13.

Say to the children that all these vessels represent the size or amount of their belief in certain areas—their self worth, their abilities, the experiences they'll have. You may explain that their belief is made up of the thoughts and feelings that something is possible or not possible for them. For example, if they ask for $100 but, in their heart, feel that they'll only get $20, that's their belief and that's what they'll get. Offer a couple of examples the children would especially relate to such as going to camp, passing a test, being accepted or invited, and so on.

On slips of paper have the children write such words

as . . . friendships, spending money, sports skill (be specific), good health, trips, nice clothing, specific abilities (piano, art, singing, typing, and so on). Select areas of concern right now for the particular child or group. Write the words for non-writers or use colored slips of paper for the categories.

Have each child decide just how much he or she really believes in that condition for himself or herself and then drop the slip of paper into the appropriately sized vessel. For instance, if they believe they can only have a couple of friends, they would put their slip titled "friendships" into a small glass. If they believe a great many friendships are possible for them, their slip would be dropped into a much larger container.

The question may come up, "How do we know what we believe?" Tell them that when we want something there is a small quiet voice within that says something like, "That's not for you—you're not worthy," or "You can do it—go for it!" That feeling or conviction is the belief that can cancel our desire or bring it to us.

Explain that when we wish more good in any area of our life, we've got to enlarge our cup of belief. We must rise above the feeling of unworthiness and know that true desires come from God.

Positive declarations or affirmations can help us start feeling worthy of greater good. Also, we might turn to God and ask to have our belief expanded. "Lord, I believe; help thou mine unbelief . . ." Mark 9:24.

The lesson might end with a guided visualization exercise. Ask the children to choose an area in which they want to expand their belief in themselves. Guide them into a state of deep relaxation and have them visualize a positive improvement in that area.

Suggested Affirmation

I am God's child and I deserve the best.

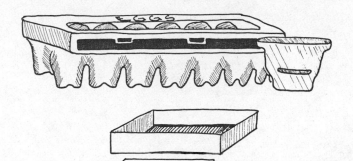

40

Separating Fear and the Problem

For older children who can write and conceptualize easily. Lesson can be divided into two parts.

Part A: Small box with a card face down in the bottom that has the word "Fear" printed on it; slips of paper; pencils.

Part B: Eggs, small cup or bowl; egg separator (a plastic gadget used to separate the yolk from the white of an uncooked egg). The egg could be separated without the separator but it would not be as visually dramatic.

──────────────Lesson──────────────

Hand the children pencils and slips of paper and request that they write down, very briefly, some of the things that have irritated or angered them in the last few days. They can put several on one slip or use more than one piece of paper. Assure them that no one will read them. When finished, have them crumple the papers and toss them into the box in the middle of the table.

Now you may explain that there is always something hidden under anger or irritation. Ask if they can guess what this emotion is. Following their responses, remove the card from the bottom of the box and display the word Fear. Offer an example or two from your own experience so they'll get the idea. You might say, "It irritated me when people told me what to do. Then I saw that the irritation was based on fear. I was fearful of others gaining control over me—of losing my freedom. Or another time it angered me when I was criticized in public. In searching for the hidden fear, I realized that I was afraid of losing friends, of being lonely."

Ask them to close their eyes and think about how their irritation or anger might have some fear hidden in it. Invite those who are willing to share examples of their anger and the fear they found under it.

Explain that any time we have a problem or challenge in life we can handle it more easily if we separate the fear from it. Hold up an egg and say: "This symbolizes a problem; I'm going to pretend it's a problem I'm having with my mother. Now I'm going to separate my fears from the problem by using this egg separator."

Place the egg separator over a cup or small bowl. Crack the egg and let the yoke fall into the center, the white into the cup. Continue with: "Watch the white, which symbolizes my fears, fall away into the cup. It feels so good to have all of that fear separated from the problem so that it doesn't even feel as if there is a problem anymore. If there are only two basic emotions, love and fear, what do you think is left in the separator after all that fear has dropped into the cup? Love, of course. Love is the absence of all negative emotion. It is unconditional acceptance. With the fear separated from the problem or challenge and just love remaining, the solution is easy. God is Love and God's Love provides the answer to any challenge in our life. We can't hear solutions when fear is in our way. Fear can block our ability to listen to Spirit within."

In a small group or home setting, each child might like the opportunity to think of a challenge and then symbolically separate the fear from it with the egg separator. Use the eggs in an omelet or for baking a treat.

Suggested
Affirmation

I am letting go of fear so as to feel more love in my life.

Just One Person
Can Lighten Darkness

Candle; matches; darkened room. Optional: candle for each child and paper-skirt wax catcher to protect hands from hot wax.

In a home setting you might light just one candle and eat by candlelight while the lesson is discussed. Observe how little light it takes to dispel darkness. Talk about how we have a choice in this world. We can choose to be just like the candle and lighten the darkness around us. Ask participants where they think that darkness might be, since they don't frequent dark rooms. Suggest that most of the darkness they will run into will be in people's minds. It can take the forms of fear, self-pity, anger, sorrow, self-doubt, jealousy, and thoughts of not having enough or of being inadequate. The children might offer specific examples of these that they've heard or seen at school or elsewhere. Ask how they can help bring light to such darkness. They may come up with saying positive things to help the other person. Discuss the ideas you and the children develop.

Explain that at times it may not be appropriate to

speak, but they can think loving thoughts about the unhappy person and picture him or her happy once again. Tell them that this picturing power is especially important when people are ill or injured. We can definitely aid them by visualizing them healthy, not as they appear to be. But we cannot decide what someone needs in order to be well or happy. We only send our loving, light-filled thoughts.

Suggest that in their prayers they might even visualize a bright, white light around the sad or ill person. This dispels darkness by creating a form of light that cannot be seen.

For additional discussion, point out how just one person with a candle can lead the way through darkness, enabling others to follow. Suggest that they can be the candlebearers and the candle they can carry is the Truth about themselves and all others. The Truth that each of us is a Child of God and made in the perfection of God can bring much light to dark minds. Offer some specific truths at their level of awareness.

Optional idea: Have each child light a small candle to show how much darkness is eliminated when several people are working together to bring light into a situation. Get suggestions as to where this light can be sent.

Suggested
Affirmation

I am a Child of God and enjoy bringing light to others.

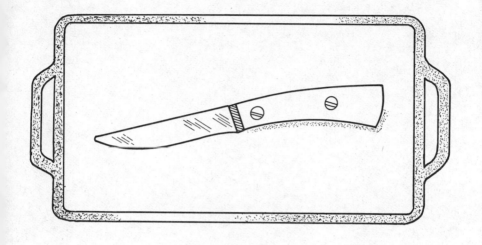

42

Anger Is
Self-Destructive

This lesson is intended for older children who are familiar with knives and not tempted to experiment with them.

Knife displayed on a tray.

—————————Lesson—————————

Ask the children how they think it would feel if someone were to pick up that knife by the blade. Then ask, "If that person were to hit someone with the handle of the knife while holding the blade, who do you think would be hurt the most?" Explain that anytime we have hate and anger, it is just like holding a knife by the blade. In fact, an author aptly said, "Hate is a weapon you wield by the blade." Such emotions really hurt the one who has them and do not touch the other person unless he or she chooses to accept them.

You may explain that anger is an attack upon oneself. It can clog the energy flow in the body. It can also create guilt that can keep people from being happy and from succeeding at what they want to do. Because of the law of attraction, more anger or hate will come into one's life. What goes out comes back after having gathered more of its kind.

Anger is God's love in us, imperfectly expressed. We can choose to redirect this energy, but first we may need to get these angry feelings out of us in an acceptable way. Some people have a firm pillow that they use as a punching bag, or when we feel full of irritation or attack feelings we can take an imaginary paper bag and blow all those nasty angry feelings into it. We can set this into an imaginery flame and let the flame consume all that negativity. A purple flame works well for this. Watching the consuming flame can be accompanied by an affirmation such as "I now let go of my anger and choose to be an expression of God's love."

Suggested Affirmation

I am a loving child of God and choose to see love in all others.

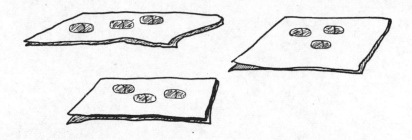

43

The Power
of the Word

Best used with older children because of the capsules.

Buy empty capsules from the druggist and fill some with a bland substance like flour, some with cayenne powder, and some with a sweet substance like sugar. Have a capsule of each kind, plus a paper plate or towel for each child.

_____Lesson_____

Hand the children a flour-filled capsule and explain that the words we use are like capsules of thought and feeling. A word is a symbol of an idea in the mind of a person. Words are creative and can form what we want or don't want depending upon the thought and feeling in them.

Now have each child empty the capsule on a paper towel or plate, explaining that this is the thought and feeling contained in a word. Invite them to moisten a finger and take a taste of the contents. Ask how it tasted and make the comparison that some of our words are also bland and don't have much creative power, (for instance, "It's nice weather today," "Let's go home," "Where'd you put the butter?"). These do not contain much feeling.

Announce that there are a couple of words that are extremely powerful. Hand out the cayenne capsules and have them dump the "thought and feeling" onto the paper towel. Again, invite them to moisten a finger and taste the contents, just a tiny bit because this word is so full of power. Get reactions about how strong, bitey, potent that substance was. Say that it represents the words "I AM." I AM is another name for God, so it is the most powerful creative statement we can say or think. Whenever we say "I AM" we bring a lot of creative power to that thought or idea.

God alway says "yes" to what we say "I AM" to, if there is a lot of feeling attached to it. When we say "I AM" with feeling, the Universe responds and that condition comes into our life. Explain that their internal speech can be just as powerful as the spoken word. It is the feelings with which we charge the words that we must watch. "I AM sick and tired of this," said with a lot of emotion, can cancel out "I AM a happy, healthy child of God" that is said without feeling. "I AM not liked" said through tears can cancel out "I AM a person others enjoy having around."

As I AM represents God in us, our spiritual self, suggest that we attach it only to positive thoughts. Encourage examples of such I AM sentences. A fun way of doing this is to play the I AM Game. For each letter of the alphabet someone offers an I AM statement (I AM aware, I AM brave, I AM creative, and so forth).

Next, give each child a third capsule (containing sugar or something else pleasant). Remind them that a word is a capsule of thought and feeling. Have them taste the contents and explain that it represents words that are sweet, loving, grateful, and uplifting.

There are no idle words. All have the power to heal or destroy. Talk about how the effect of words stay with us long after the sound of the word is gone. They may wish to share some words they remember that have helped or hurt weeks later.

Discuss words they might use that will leave people better than when they found them. Encourage them to use only words that represent the very best thinking of which they are capable. End the lesson by speaking some uplifting words to each other—words of appreciation and gratitude.

Suggested Affirmation

The most powerful words I can say are I AM.

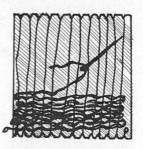

Weaving Our Spiritual Consciousness

Best used with older children who have developed some spiritual concepts.

Materials

Each child and the adult should have either a piece of sturdy hardware cloth (wire mesh) with the edges bound by tape *or* a piece of cardboard with string wrapped around it to form a warp. Small notches in the cardboard will keep the string in place. Have lengths of yarn in a variety of colors and large-eyed plastic yarn needles. An alternative to a needle is wrapping the last inch of yarn with about an inch of masking or cellophane tape, and cutting at an angle to make a point. If you wish to prepare the yarn ahead of time, the ends can be dipped into melted wax or white glue. A bobby pin is another needle alternative.

Lesson

Explain that the piece of hardware cloth or cardboard represents their individual consciousness—their collection of thoughts and feeling—their total awareness (sometimes called the soul). You might then say, "We are going to talk about our spiritual awareness—the thoughts and feelings we have about God and other spiritual matters. These are the thoughts that are woven into our consciousness and build our particular spiritual character. Sometimes we're not even aware of what our spiritual beliefs are, so let's try to identify them. We'll use these pieces of yarn to represent our thoughts, and we'll weave them into our consciousness (hold up the warp). Let's first weave in our beliefs about God. I'm going to use this pretty purple yarn for my belief about God."

At this point encourage the children to choose a piece of yarn to represent their ideas about God and to thread it through the needle or wrap tape around the end. As they weave it in and out of the warp, get them to verbalize their idea of God—the feelings they have about what God is or is not. You may choose to begin by sharing your idea of God (for instance, Love, the One Power, all knowing, present throughout the Universe and in everyone and everything, the One Creator, not a person, too vast to understand, and so forth). Each concept about God could be a different strand if so desired.

Don't let any of the topics discussed turn into a guessing game where there is only one answer acceptable to you. This is a beautiful opportunity to hear their ideas and these may not come out if they feel they are being judged. In other words, don't make it a right-or-wrong game, but an opportunity to note where you may wish to offer instruction later. Sharing your thoughts without being critical of theirs may be the best approach.

Next ask them to select a piece of yarn to represent who they think they are—their spiritual identity (for instance, a child of God; a spiritual, mental, and physical being; a Holy Son or Daughter of God; a part of God as a drop of water is part of the ocean; an expression of God; an inheritor of spiritual gifts; a unique and special being; and so forth).

If the youngsters are old enough, they may choose

to exercise their design ability as the yarn is woven in. The results could be lovely.

Have the next strand of yarn represent their idea of why they are here—the purpose of their life. Responses could include: becoming my real self—the perfect person God created me to be; performing my part in God's plan— my special function; expressing God in my own unique way; learning the lessons that I have chosen to learn in this lifetime; being truly helpful.

The subject of our immortality or beliefs about death might follow next (for instance, there is no birth or death for the soul; life is eternal and we just change costumes, we can choose to live in many bodies in order to become as perfect as God wants us to be; death is a joyous experience). Again, have them weave in a strand depicting their particular belief system.

The next subject area might deal with the nature of the Universe or the world in which we live (for instance, everything in the Universe operates by Law and Order, cause and effect; thoughts become things; we create our experience by our thinking and feeling; there is only one power—God, the Good, and so forth.).

Continue eliciting thoughts on other spiritual topics (prayer, meditation, the Bible, heaven, Jesus Christ, Holy Spirit, love, or whatever you deem significant). Weave the yarn strands into the form called "consciousness."

When finished, admire together the results, reminding them that each strand represents a spiritual idea and that this is how spiritual character is built. With older children you may wish to explain that consciousness precedes experience. The more that spiritual understanding is built into their consciousness, the better will be their life experiences.

One of the best ways to expand consciousness or increase spiritual awareness is through meditation. Meditation is listening to God, whereas prayer is talking to God. You may wish to end the lesson with a time of silent meditation so that each may receive his or her own guidance from God.

Note: If the youngsters are old enough, they may wish to make a "legend" to tape on the back of the weaving to remind them of which color yarn they used for what topic. Key words to remind them of their ideas might be added also. The finished product could be hung on their bedroom wall.

Suggested Affirmation

I am growing in awareness as I give time each day to listen to God for guidance.

Index

Risks, 97
Role-playing, 122
Rubber bands, 43, 105

S

Salt, 13
Salt shaker, 33, 51, 163
Sand, 13
Sauce dishes, 91
Saucer, 13
Scissors, 33, 51, 83
Scouring pad, 33
Security, 1
Self-esteem, 1, 2, 9, 113, 114
Sink, 47
Soap, 51
Soul, 207
Soup, cans of, 51, 115
Spice can, 33
Spice jars, 51
Spirit, 136, 157, 185, 190
   everywhere present, 27–30
   guidance of, 121–22
   individualization of, 73, 74
   visible form of, 19–22
   See also God
Spiritual consciousness, 207–12
Sponges, 91
Spoons, 37, 47, 69, 121
Stones, 157
Strainer, 69
Straws, 33, 37, 173
String, 51, 73, 97, 151
Subconscious mind, 8, 9, 167–69
Substance, 131–32
Sugar, 203

T

Tape, 33, 51, 63, 167, 207
Tea, 69
Tea kettle, 22
Teaspoons, 77, 101, 163
Tension, 105
Thankfulness, 13–14
Thimble, 185
Thoughts, 87, 207
   atmosphere of, 67–70
   becoming things, 129–32
   choosing, 115–18
   contained in words, 203–5
   experience and, 61–65
   friendly, 43

Thoughts (*continued*)
   as gifts, 133–36
   light-filled, 196
   magnetic, 33–34
   monitoring, 163–64
   positive, 37–39, 45–48
   source of, 53–56
   words as symbols of, 59
Timer, 157
Toothpicks, 33
Tray, 199
Truth, 1, 2, 4, 7, 196
Turkey baster, 113
Typing paper, 55, 123

U

Understanding, 101
Unhappiness, 34, 63–64
Universal substance, 83
Universe, 211
Unworthiness, feelings of, 186

V

Vibrations of emotions, 56
Visible form of spirit, 19–22
Visible world, 173–75
Visualization, 8, 9, 26, 84, 136, 159, 186, 196
Voice for God, 179–81

W

Walnuts, 157
Wastebasket, 147
Water, 21, 37, 47, 91, 113, 121, 157, 163, 173
Water colors, 132
Waxed paper, 151
Wire, 51
Wire coat hangers, 151
Wire mesh, 207
Wisdom, 29, 101, 126, 127
Wooden spoon, 121
Words, 87, 161–64
   power of, 201–5
   uplifting, 57–60

Y

Yarn, 151, 207
Yarn needles, 207
Yo-Yo, 43, 44